KABBALAH CENTRE BOOKS

The Zohar *24 volumes by Rabbi Shimon bar Yohai, The cardinal work in the literature of Kabbalah. Original Aramaic text with Hebrew translation and commentary by Rabbi Yehudah Ashlag*

Miracles, Mysteries, and Prayer Volume II, Rabbi Berg (also available in Spanish and Russian)

Kabbalah for the Layman Volume I, Rabbi Berg (also available in Hebrew, Spanish, French, Russian, Italian, German, Persian, Chinese and Portuguese)

Kabbalah for the Layman Volumes II, III, Rabbi Berg (also available in Hebrew, Spanish, French and Italian)

Wheels of a Soul Rabbi Berg (also available in Hebrew, Spanish, French, Russian, Italian, and Persian)

Astrology: The Star Connection, The Science of Judaic Astrology Rabbi Berg (also available in Hebrew, Spanish, French and Persian)

Time Zones: Creating Order from Chaos Rabbi Berg (also available in French, Spanish, Hebrew and Persian)

To The Power of One Rabbi Berg (also available in French and Spanish)

Power of the Aleph Beth Volumes I, II, Rabbi Berg (also available in Hebrew, French and Spanish)

The Kabbalah Connection Rabbi Berg (also available in Spanish and Hebrew)

Kabbalistik Astrology Made Easy Rabbi Berg in French Translation

Gift of the Bible Rabbi Yehudah Ashlag, Foreword by Rabbi Berg (also available in French, Hebrew and Spanish)

Zohar: Parashat Pinhas Volumes I, II, III, Translated , compiled and edited by Rabbi Berg (also available in Spanish)

An Entrance to the Tree of Life Rabbi Yehudah Ashlag, Compiled and edited by Rabbi Berg (also available in Spanish)

Ten Luminous Emanations Rabbi Yehudah Ashlag, Volumes I, II, Compiled and edited by Rabbi Berg (also available in Hebrew , 7 Volume set)

An Entrance to The Zohar Rabbi Yehudah Ashlag, Compiled and edited by Rabbi Berg

General Principles of Kabbalah Rabbi M. Luzzatto (also available in Italian)

Light of Redemption by Rabbi Levi Krakovsky

Kabbalistik Children's Stories:

Heaven on Your Head, Tales of the Enlightened, Legends of Israel, Legends of Zion DR. S. Z. Kahana

---

SOON TO BE PUBLISHED

Secret Codes of the Universe Rabbi Berg

Kabbalistik Astrology Made Easy Rabbi Berg

Ten Luminous Emanations Volumes III, IV, Rabbi Yehudah Ashlag , compiled and edited by Rabbi Berg

Miracles, Mysteries, and Prayer Volume I, II, Rabbi Berg, in French Translation

Time Zones: Creating Order from Chaos Rabbi Berg, in Russian Translation

To The Power of One Rabbi Berg, in Russian Translation

Gift of the Bible Rabbi Yehudah Ashlag, Foreword by Rabbi Berg, in Russian Translation

BOOKS AND TAPES AVAILABLE
AT BOOKSELLERS AND KABBALAH CENTRES AROUND THE WORLD

MIRACLES, MYSTERIES, AND PRAYER

VOLUME ONE

MIRACLES, MYSTERIES, AND PRAYER

VOLUME ONE

RABBI BERG

FIRST PRINTING
April 1993
SECOND PRINTING
July 1995

0-924457-83-X (Soft Cover)

For further information:

THE KABBALAH LEARNING CENTRE
83-84 115th Street, Richmond Hill
NEW YORK, 11418
Tel. (718) 805-9122

— or —

P.O. BOX 14168
THE OLD CITY, JERUSALEM

PRINTED IN U.S.A.
1995

Perhaps
you took this book
because you were curious.
Or,
perhaps you have to work
for something.
Or,
maybe you took it
to prove
this book is wrong.
But,
by the time you are finished,
You will be challenged!

For my wife,
Karen,
In the vastness of cosmic space
and infinity of lifetimes,
it is my bliss
to share with you,
my soulmate,
the Age of Aquarius.

ABOUT THE CENTRES

Kabbalah is mystical Judaism. It is the deepest and most hidden meaning of the Torah, or Bible. Through the ultimate knowledge and mystical practices of Kabbalah one can reach the highest spiritual levels attainable. Many people rely on belief, faith and dogma in pursuing the meaning of life, the unknown and the unseen. Yet, Kabbalists seek a spiritual connection with the Creator and the forces of the Creator. The strange thus becomes familiar, and faith becomes knowledge.

Throughout history, those who knew and practiced the Kabbalah were extremely careful in their dissemination of the knowledge — for they knew the masses of mankind had not yet been prepared for the ultimate truth of existence. Today Kabbalists know that it is not only proper, but necessary, to make the Kabbalah available to all who seek it.

The Kabbalah Learning Centre is an independent, non-profit institute founded in Israel in 1922. The Centre provides research, information and assistance to those who seek the insights of Kabbalah. The Centre offers public lectures, classes, seminars and excursions to mystical sites at branches in Israel — in Jerusalem, Tel Aviv, Haifa, Beer Sheva — and in the United States in New York and Los Angeles. Branches have been opened in Mexico, Toronto, Florida, North Miami, Paris, and London. Thousands of people have benefited by the Centre's activities. The publication of its Kabbalistic material continues to be the most comprehensive of its kind in the world. It includes translations in English, Hebrew, Russian, German, Portuguese, French, Spanish, Farsi (Persian) and Chinese.

Kabbalah can provide true meaning in one's being and the knowledge necessary for one's ultimate benefit. It can point towards a spirituality beyond belief. The Research Centre of Kabbalah will continue to make the Kabbalah available to all those who seek it.

ABOUT THE ZOHAR

The ZOHAR, the basic source of the Kabbalah was written by Rabbi Shimon bar Yoḥai while in hiding from the Romans in a cave in Pe'quin for 13 years. It was later brought to light by Rabbi Moses de Leon in Spain, and further revealed through the Safed Kabbalists and the Lurianic system of Kabbalah.

The programs of the Research Centre of Kabbalah have been established to provide opportunities for learning, teaching, research and demonstration of specialized knowledge drawn from the ageless wisdom of the Zohar and the Jewish Sages. Long kept from the masses, today this knowledge should be shared by all who seek to understand the deeper meaning of our Jewish heritage, a more profound meaning of life. Modern science is only beginning to discover what our Sages veiled in symbolism. This knowledge is of a very practical nature and can be applied daily for the betterment of our lives and of humankind.

Our courses and materials deal with the Zoharic understanding of each weekly portion of the Torah. Every facet of Jewish life is covered and other dimensions, hitherto unknown, provide a deeper connection to a superior Reality. Three important introductory courses cover such aspects as: Time, Space and Motion; Reincarnation, Marriage, Divorce, Kabbalistic Meditation, Limitation of the five senses, Illusion-Reality, Four Phases, Male and Female, Death, Sleep, Dreams; Food: what is kosher and why; Circumcision, Redemption of the First Born, *Shatnes, Shabbat.*

Darkness cannot prevail in the presence of Light. A darkened room must respond even to the lighting of a candle. As we share this moment together we are beginning to witness a people's revolution of enlightenment. And indeed, some of us are already participating in it. The darkened clouds of strife and conflict will make their presence felt only as long as the Eternal Light remains concealed.

The Zohar now remains a final, if not the only, solution to infusing the cosmos with the revealed Light of the Force. The Zohar is not a book about religion. Rather, the Zohar is concerned with the relationship between the unseen forces of the cosmos, the Force and Its impact on Man.

The Zohar promises that, with the ushering in of the Age of Aquarius, the cosmos will become readily accessible to human understanding. It states, that in the days of the Messiah, "there will no longer be the necessity for one to request of his neighbor, teach me wisdom" (Zohar III, p.58a). "One day they will no longer teach every man his neighbor and every man his brother, saying know the Lord. For they shall all know Me, from the youngest to the oldest of them" (Jeremiah 31:34).

We can and must regain control of our lives and environment. To achieve this objective the Zohar provides us with an opportunity to transcend the crushing weight of universal negativity.

The daily perusing of the Zohar, without any attempt at translation or "understanding" will fill our consciousness with the Light, improving our well-being and influencing everything in our environment toward positive attitudes. Even the scanning of the Zohar by those unfamiliar with the Hebrew Aleph Beth will accomplish the same result.

The connection that we establish through scanning the Zohar is a connection and unity with the Light of the Lord. The letters, even if we do not consciously know Hebrew or Aramaic, are the channels through which the connection is made. They could be likened to the dialing of the right telephone number, or the typing in the right codes to run a computer program. The connection is established at the metaphysical level of our being and radiates into our physical plane of existence...but first the metaphysical "mending" must take place. Through positive thoughts and actions we have to consciously permit the immense power of the Zohar to radiate love, harmony and peace into our lives — for us to share with all of humanity and the universe.

As we enter the years ahead, the Zohar will continue to be a people's book, striking a sympathetic chord in the hearts and minds of those who long for peace, truth and relief from suffering. In the face of crises and catastrophe it has the ability to resolve agonizing human afflictions by restoring each individual's relationship with the Force.

ABOUT THE AUTHOR

RABBI BERG is Dean of the Research Centre of Kabbalah. Born in New York City, into a family descended from a long line of Rabbis, he is an ordained Orthodox Rabbi (from the renowned rabbinical seminary Torat VaDaat). While traveling to Israel in 1962, he met his teacher, the distinguished Kabbalist Rabbi Yehudah Zvi Brandwein, student of Rabbi Yehudah Ashlag Z"L and then Dean of the Research Centre of Kabbalah. During that period the Centre expanded substantially with the establishment of the United States branch in 1965 through which it currently disseminates and distributes its publications. Rabbi Berg did research at the Centre under the auspices of his beloved teacher Rabbi Brandwein Z"L, writing books on such topics as the origins of Kabbalah, creation, cosmic consciousness, energy, and the myths of the speed of light and the light barrier. Following the death of his master in 1969, Rabbi Berg assumed the position of Dean of the Centre. He expanded its publication program through the translation of source material on the Kabbalah into English and other languages. Rabbi Berg moved with his devoted and dedicated wife Karen to Israel in 1971, where they opened the doors of the Centre to all seekers of self identity. They established centres in all major cities throughout Israel, while at the same time lecturing at the City University of Tel Aviv. They returned to the United States in 1981 to further found centres of learning in major cities all over the world. In addition to publishing scientific and popular articles, Rabbi Berg is the author, translator and/or editor of eighteen other books, including the *Kabbalah for the Layman* series, *Wheels of a Soul*, and *Time Zones*.

ACKNOWLEDGEMENTS

I would like to express my gratitude to Roy Tarlow for compiling, reviewing and editing the manuscript. He made fundamental and frequent contributions to the essential ideas and their connections to the overall style. The delight I found in our many discussions is one of my principal rewards from this book. Many heartfelt thanks to him for his helpful suggestions and careful proofreading of the manuscript.

TABLE OF CONTENTS

*Four fundamental elements expressed by the planets;
the internal energy-intelligence of the celestial bodies
and their relationship to Man; the Force as the primal life flow divided into ten Sfirot; the contributions of the patriarch Abraham and Rabbi Isaac
Luria toward our understanding of the purpose and
influences of the planets.*

*A comprehensive road map and knowledge provide
the connection to control of our life.*

*The physicists' quantum picture of the universe; the
background-figure illusion and its implications; the
physicists' fruitless search for the quantum reality; the
Divine word of infinity transformed into finite language by the Kabbalist.*

*The question of causality in classical physics and
Kabbalah; Rabbi Ashlag's contributions to the study
of nature's laws; is the Universe expanding? Matter
and anti-matter; the creative process according to
Kabbalah; the effect of man's thought and the
Encircling Light; parallel universes.*

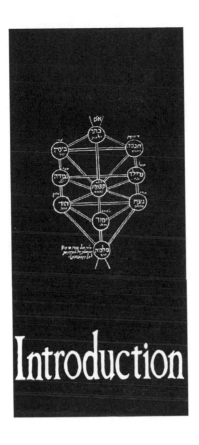

Introduction

IN THIS AGE OF AQUARIUS WE ARE ALL ON A JOURNEY towards expanded awareness. We are all on this path, whether our conscious mind agrees or not. Slowly, but surely, the clouds of illusion become thinner and less imposing. For, at the end of our journey, at last there is only the true basic reality: Light.

Astrology is essentially an ancient science, however, its popularization is new. It is no longer one of the esoteric sciences with its wisdom, knowledge and practice limited to the select few. In the dawning of the Age of Aquarius, respected scientists have gone public with theories that propose a scientific basis for the ancient practice of astrology. British astronomer Percy Seymour reveals some interesting evidence that the planets and signs of our constellation do indeed influence our lives.

There is disagreement among astrologers as to when the

Aquarian Age began. Rabbi Abraham Azulai calculates the transitional influence of Aquarius to be in the early part of the 16th century, recognizing the Ari, Rabbi Isaac Luria, as the harbinger of the Messianic Age. Thus, the essence of universal harmony was, and is, the single thread that weaves through Lurianic teachings.

Kabbalistic astrology is astronomy with an explanation as to why celestial bodies appear and behave the way they do. The *Book of Formation* has brought to earth astronomy as it applies to the affairs of man. The limited science of astronomy is concerned with discovering the nature of the heavenly, celestial bodies. Astrology explores and determines their influence on our lives.

Not surprisingly, the astronomy community, entrenched in fossilized ideas concerning astrology, denounces its teachings and damns anyone who espouses them. Although both astronomy and astrology take their names from the stars, they appear to hold

nothing else in common. However, nothing could be further from the truth. Granted that astronomy is concerned with discovering the nature of heavenly bodies, is there something wrong in asking why their behavior is expressed in such a manner? This is the function of Kabbalistic Astrology.

With an uncertainty principle penetrating the very fibre of the science of physics, scientific justification can only be marginal. In addition, once the idea or notion behind celestial movement has been ascertained, physical expression or manifestation becomes secondary. Careful and detailed observations of the changing positions of the planets against the background of fixed stars become an unnecessary if not futile exercise. Observations can be and are misleading.

Although science has long given up on reaching metaphysical causes of celestial movement, the *Book of Formation* is replete with this important data. The irony is, that this information has been with us for over 3400 years, and yet, has never

caught the eye or fancy of the scientific establishment.

Strong evidence exists to support some aspects of astrology and the way these affect human life despite the absence of any mechanism to explain how celestial bodies affect life in the universe. Magnetic fields of activity pervade our universe. Before the evidence began to emerge (as if it did not already exist), the existence of magnetic activity was well known to the Kabbalist. "There is no blade of grass below that does not have an astral spirit or force from above," declares the Zohar[1].

The physical agencies that channel the astral influence are the individual celestial magnetic signals that emanate from the cosmos. Magnetic signals vary from day to day and even hour to hour. The problem that scientists face is how to read the information and what it means to the average person.

That magnetism pervades the entire universe, just as gravity does, has long been known to science. The entire earth is a magnet with a south and a north pole surrounded by a magnetic field 30 times larger than the planet itself. The Milky Way's magnetic field extends for millions of light years through space.

Human beings respond to the magnetism or magnetic fields of other human beings. This idea found its way into the Babylonian Talmud with its declaration that "everyone has a magnetic field that extends approximately 7 1/2 feet through space.[2]"

The fetus in a womb will receive magnetic signals from the prevailing planets and signs of the constellation. When the baby is ready to be born, it awaits a magnetic signal from the configuration of celestial entities which then triggers the moment of birth. We must bear in mind that physical magnetic signals from the cosmos are merely the physical expressions of an internal, metaphysical intelligence of these celestial bodies.

Now, what determines the exact moment of birth, and more importantly, why this fetus will breathe its first breath of life now, while others will do so moments later, has, up to the present time, remained a mystery. Conventional astrology defines and labels the magnetic effects of the cosmos. By crediting the astral influences with the power to affect and predict personality traits and future events, astrology penetrates the internal energy-intelligence of the cosmos and its effect upon the internal composite of individuals.

To consider and rely on the magnetic fields as the determining phase and factor of human behavior will, as in the past, remain an exercise in futility. Physical expressions are the result of human thought and not the other way around. Only an idiot proceeds to build a high-rise structure without prior thought and planning. The metaphysical thought-intelligence precedes any subsequent physical manifestation.

The question as to why Jerusalem is referred to as the Holy City is followed by the typical answer, "because the Holy Temple was located there." The Kabbalistic response, of necessity, follows the doctrine that the Holy Temple, a physical manifestation, was located in Jerusalem as a direct response to the internal, metaphysical energy center to be found in Jerusalem. The Holy Temple functioned as a channel for the intense energy that existed in Jerusalem. Jerusalem then was the primary cause for the Temple locating in its midst.[3]

Magnetic fields, too, are the result of an internal dynamic interplay between the energy-intelligences of celestial bodies. Their physical relationships and interactions are in response to an internal mechanism that is governed by a metaphysical calendar.

The calendar is the metaphysical road map of astrology. The celestial bodies are the channels.

The question that must be raised is, who or what governs and directs the particular internal intelligences of celestial bodies that astronomers observe in the path and motion of these bodies? The Kabbalistic response to our inquiry is contained within the coded packets of energy known as *Sfirot.* Celestial bodies and their movements are manipulated by these *Sfirot* to express the internal energy of seven *Sfirot.* Consequently, there arose the necessity for our seven planets to become the administering executors by generating forces in certain patterns which are responsible for universal behavior.

Therefore, from time to time, the planets fall into striking geometric patterns. Sometimes, they queue up in a line or square off at right angles to one another and at other times gang up on one side of the sun. Early astrologers came to recognize their strange power and named their aspects. They observed that certain planetary aspects in the heavens coincided with significant events that took place on earth. After considerable observation, they concluded that changes in planetary positions altered and brought about changes in magnetic fields. They then were able to use this information to predict future events.

The celestial bodies, therefore, exert the precise and proper energy-intelligent force necessary at the actual moment of birth. What determines the moment of birth depends upon the incarnated printout of former lifetimes. We all return for the purpose of *Tikune* or correction.

To ensure an exact frame of mind, psychologically and otherwise, the moment of birth which stamps and impresses the essential characteristics, of necessity coincides with the positions of celestial bodies and their dynamic interplay with each other. The collective internal consciousness of these celestial entities, is then channeled and provides the metaphysical as well as physical expressions of all universal life forms.

Past lifetimes set the personality on course, determining which planetary signal will herald an individual's birth. Astrology merely labels what prior incarnations have already ordained. Cause and effect on one level will produce everything in accordance with this universal law. Other elements, however, can alter the entire existence or composition of the effect.

Astrology is a science that provides us with predictable information coinciding with the aspect of fate along the lines of Newtonian classical physics. When we consider the aspect of achieving another level of consciousness, we are not rejecting science. We are merely taking in the broader spectrum of things extant at the more subtle, subatomic level to alter the same universal law of cause and effect.

The law of *Tikune* is a continuous experience because, so long as *Tikune* is not achieved, we can safely state that the universal law of cause and effect will prevail. However, once we have ascended the spiritual ladder which is the path to achieving *Tikune* (correcting the faults and flaws of prior incarnations), the celestial bodies or stars no longer compel. That is, stars impel, but do not compel after correction.

The point being made here is that the knowledge of astrology enables the individual to provide a rational explanation of life and its mysteries based on the law of cause and effect.

Thus, the Kabbalistic view of astrology is dramatically

different from the conventional pursuit of the science. Conventional astrology contends that the individual will take a course of action because of the arrangement of the stars, whereas Kabbalah contends the *Tikune* process places the individual in an astrological position so that the stars will impel him into the needed direction.

Are birth charts a pictorial view of the metaphysical interface or merely the result of a physically expressed view of a predictable future? For example, if the moment of birth is hastened forward in time by labor-inducing drugs or delivery by caesarean section, astrology considers the moment of birth to be the right moment of birth. The Kabbalists claim the physical intervention or invasion by the physician was prompted by the interface printout of former lifetimes. Although medical interference prevented the planetary positions from determining the time of birth, this does not mean that the time of birth occurred at an astrologically wrong time. Regardless of the physical surroundings, hospital, doctor, etc. the time of birth was determined by the former lifetime's printout, and thus, the moment of birth was astrologically the right time.

The Kabbalistic viewpoint maintains that physical entities or circumstances in no way determine or affect the prior metaphysical realm. It is rather this unknowable, non-material realm that contains the determining internal cosmic energy force that ultimately will make manifest the particular channels of energy by which the space-time energy field becomes a reality.

Celestial bodies simply represent the life-giving forces, the internal or external stimulation in any given area of life.

In brief, the stars determine nothing. The basic destiny pattern is considered fundamentally unalterable. Therefore, when we have a sequence of experiences which the natal chart could predict with 100 percent accuracy, it is our own incarnation we are dealing with. This is the reason why the birth occurred at a particular time in a particular country under the particular astral and geographical influences of that given moment.

For all the inviolability of the basic destiny pattern, however, we have a degree of freedom almost without limitation. The natal chart reveals the blinders and restrictions that will keep us from becoming and feeling free. These blinders are of our own manufacture. We built them in prior lifetimes, but because we created them, we can break them and ascend to a higher level of consciousness.

This higher level of consciousness obviously will come about through a higher form of meditation and living an ideal spiritual life. Then, and only then, can we truly be liberated from the pattern of destiny that seems so unalterable. Then we can ascend and alter the initial natal chart.

The moment of birth is not a random event. As the soul travels through the metaphysical space between the endless and mundane worlds, it passes through various levels of energies, picking up what is required, both of good and bad influences in terms of habits and attitudes carried over from the totality of its previous incarnations.

The planets then are symbols of more than merely physical dimensions. Their placement, at the moment of birth, can be compared to a program entered into a computer, except that this computer is as massive as the billions of stars and planets of which it is constructed. What emerges is the "software" of the individual's present life with the good and the evil, the strength and the weakness, of previous lives neatly formulated from the eternal computer's memory bank.

The importance of the placement of the planetary and astral bodies for that purpose is no less than the importance of all the binary bits of information necessary to construct the program sought for a terrestrial computer. The moment of birth is specifically designed to assure that the individual arrives in this life with every bit of the baggage he accumulated in the last one. The soul without baggage obviously would have no reason to return.

When an individual is born on a particular day, the Kabbalistic astrologer is given an easily read blueprint of that person's psyche. More importantly, along with the blueprint, comes the knowledge of how the individual may be able to alter the inborn program, create another and thus escape the chains of predestination.

It is precisely in this area of free will that this book will differ from other books on astrology. The natal chart need not be on a collision course with free will. The person who relaxes before reaching his limit is an unhappy failure. One who explores the limits of one's capacity will be a success. The purpose of this book is to provide the software necessary to enhance the wellbeing of humanity, that for so long has suffered the predictable events of chaos and disorder.

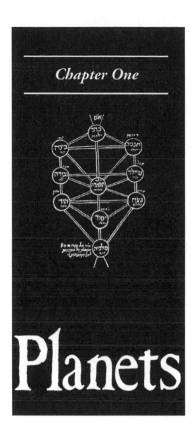

Chapter One

Planets

PLANETS INITIALLY WERE DETECTED IN ANTIQUITY AS visual objects that wander across the night sky in a time period of months or years. These driftings were known to Abraham, the Patriarch, author of the *Book of Formation* some 3,800 years ago. He knew all the naked-eye planets: Saturn (*Shabtai*), Jupiter (*Tzedek*), Mars (*Madim*), Venus (*Nogah*), Mercury (*Kokhav*), Sun (*Ḥama*) and Moon (*Levanah*). Planets were thus identified because of their forward-thrust nature as translated from the original Aramaic description *Zion Kokhvai Lekhet*[4], (the seven forward thrusting stars).

Early Kabbalists were intimately familiar with the celestial bodies and regarded their movements across the heavens as physical expressions of extraterrestrial intelligence. They viewed the constellations and planets as intelligent entities, motivated by

internal energies which manifest on Earth as the four elements —
water, fire, air and earth. These four fundamental elements are
the consciousness levels by which man, animal, vegetation and
inanimate kingdoms function. The planets are motivated by the
internal energy-intelligences of the four elements.

Let us explore the Kabbalistic perspective of the energy-
intelligences that exert their influence over every facet of our existence. The Sun and Moon exert the most direct influence over
earth's inhabitants.[5] The astral influences of the planetary bodies,
Saturn, Jupiter, Mars, Venus and Mercury also affect us, but to a
lesser degree. Through Kabbalistic astrology we become aware of
how these cosmic intelligences operate, affect us, and of how to
make use of them.

Their observations of the universe, drawn from the various reflections of the Zohar, enabled them to provide a valid
guide for the individual in search of *total* understanding of the
self. Furthermore, and more importantly, they provided a discipline for universal human behavior, taking the individual to a
higher level of consciousness and consequently to a higher level
of moral conduct.

There can never be a better world for people to live in
until there are better people in it. Through astrology, the individual becomes aware of his internal intelligent cosmic force. The
internal knowledge of astrology, which was lost and yet revealed
in the *Book of Formation*, stressed the point that whenever any
movement in the music of the universe is noted, there is some
internal metaphysical force that has brought it about to be sensed
and, at times, actually seen.

The principal members of the sun's family are the planets
Mercury, Venus, Mars, Jupiter, Saturn and the celestial body, the

Moon. The Sun, the Moon and the five naked-eye planets were known to antiquity. However, on the night of March 13th, 1781 William Herschel discovered the planet Uranus. The discovery of the next planet, Neptune, was made in Berlin by a German astronomer named Johann Galle on the night of September 23rd, 1846.

And then we come to Pluto, the furthest known outpost of the solar system which was discovered in March of 1930. Pluto pursues its lonely path around the sun and takes approximately 248 years for the journey as opposed to earth's journey of one year. Mercury, the smallest planet and the one closest to the sun makes a single revolution around the sun in a little less than 88 earthly days, and thus completes the trip four times in one of our years.

It is interesting to note at this stage that the latter three planets were not considered to have any direct influence on earth's inhabitants. The Kabbalistic astrologer did not include the astral influences of Uranus, Pluto and Neptune in determining the extent of our position relative to the scheme of the universe. This idea conflicts with contemporary astrologers who, when faced with the discovery of these three new planets, revised the relationship between the planets and signs of the constellation or zodiac. This subject shall be dealt with more fully in a later chapter.

The universe and our existence are based on a set of laws which have been slowly revealed to man since the beginning of mankind. If we would only learn how to live according to these laws, man's understanding would grow and his pain and suffering would become increasingly less.

Man's ability to decipher a part of the universe's master

plan has been greatly enhanced with the approaching Age of Aquarius.[6] The human race must and will evolve to be able to incorporate these new vibrations into its collective consciousness. However, the internal energy-intelligences of our celestial bodies will not and should not change with new discoveries or our developed comprehension of their existence. Designer's clothes may change from year to year. The truth does not.

Thus, some of the doctrines contained within astrology's "inner sanctum" are now permitted to be presented to the masses. With an Aquarian consciousness we are presently in a position to begin to understand and use them. The well-spring of information contained in the Patriarch Abraham's *Book of Formation* will establish these eternal truths which do not change and are not gone with the wind.

Kabbalistic astrologers-astronomers knew and understood that planetary influences are nothing more than bodies of energy. The planets thus are symbols of more than merely physical dimensions. The Kabbalist raises the important question as to "why" the planets locate in the heavens as they do. Of what significance is the astronomer's findings if they do not relate to man's ability to develop the faculties to use this wisdom in daily life.

The Force is the primal life flow that is filtered up and down from one level to another. This idea is noted by the code name "The Line."[7] The Line serves to conceptually illuminate the Force in a linear dimension. The Force then becomes transformed from a circular, infinite state to a condition of limitation. Mankind can now grasp, with his finite mind, the myriad of energy-intelligences which express the Force as separate manifestations.

The Force is always present in all its glory. We, the viewer, do not see it and are unaware that it even exists. There is no disappearance in the realm of the metaphysical. Essential changes only occur within material objects and in the perceptions of man. Yet, it is the same One Force expressing itself in an infinite multitude of forms and intensities.

The real world, the level of infinity, is unified. In fact, there is an aspect of unity within the atmosphere, within us, within everything that exists in this world. This Circular Condition is indicated on the physical level by the planets which are approximately spherical, the atom, air bubbles, the concentric circles that form around a pebble in the water, as well as the human head, eye, mouth and face.

The same may be said of the seed that grew into a tree. The same may be said of the Force that turned into planets. As with all phases of emanation or process of development, the Force is subdivided into ten Sfirotic components.[8] The word *Sfirah* signifies brightness and infinite luminosity contained as packets or encapsulated forms of energy.

Hence, we find the planets as circular objects consisting of the ten sfirotic components of the Force. Consequently, our universe consists of ten planets each representing a unique and particular aspect of the Force, each distinctively circular and occupying its peculiar position within the galaxy. The upper three *Sfirot* are known by their code names *Keter* (Crown), *Hokmah* (Wisdom) and *Binah* (Intelligence). These three packets of energy are referred to as the Head, connected with the great Circle of Infinity. The lower seven *Sfirot* alone are susceptible to the friction and pitfalls of finite existence, our mundane existence.

It was the contention of the Ari, Rabbi Isaac Luria, that the true nature of existence is unified, timeless and perfectly still.

What the Kabbalist means when we are told that this world is an illusion is that the circular aspect of existence is infinite, but all aspects of worldly existence, having a beginning, middle, and end, are finite, and therefore, imperfect.

It is precisely for this reason that Pluto, Neptune and Uranus are located so distantly away from the epicenter of our solar system, the Sun. Uranus travels around the Sun in eighty-four years. Neptune, farther away, takes approximately one hundred sixty-four years. And finally, Pluto, the farthest known outpost of our solar system, takes approximately two hundred and forty-eight years to complete its journey around the Sun.

The origins of the study of astronomy are lost in the mists of time. Furthermore, we know that the astronomer understood little of the whys and wherefores of it all. Indeed, the daily struggle, simply to see and know what lies up there in the distant heavens, left him little time to ponder any further. To say the least, had the knowledge of Kabbalah been as widespread then as it is today, the science of astronomy might have moved beyond the task of simply knowing what lies out there and ventured into the *whys* of our universe.

Let us take as our starting point the lines from the opening chapter of the *Book of Formation* written more than 3,800 years ago.

> Ten are the numbers out of nothing. Ten, not nine and ten not eleven .... The three primal elements, water, fire and air are typified by a balance .... The seven double letters shall as it were symbolize wisdom, wealth, fruitfulness, life, dominion, peace and beauty. These become manifest in the universe by the seven planets, Saturn, Jupiter,

Mars, Sun, Venus, Mercury and Moon.[9]

The three outer planets of Uranus, Neptune and Pluto symbolize the three essential elements of our universe. As such, they represent the three fundamental energy-intelligences of water, fire and air, or right, left and central columns.[10] Therefore, these three planets were not included as astral-influencing celestial bodies due to their *unmanifested* state of consciousness. Despite their expression as physical, material entities, nonetheless, this physical manifestation is, Kabbalistically, considered illusionary. Astral influences cannot be established by the way they are observed in the world we experience.[11] This then, explains their position in the heavens and additionally their length of journey around the Sun.

Let us begin by examining the time these planets take to journey around the Sun. You will notice that Uranus and Neptune *together* travel approximately two hundred forty-eight years in their journey. Strange as it seems, Pluto's journey around the Sun also takes two hundred-forty eight years. For the Kabbalist, the numerical value of two hundred forty-eight provides a coded significance regarding the Force or source of energy in our universe.[12]

If there were any other number to describe the three outer- most planets we'd say "So what?" But 248 stands out. What we are talking about is the raw naked energy contained in empty space. To most people empty space should be truly empty, a vacuum, an absolute nothing. To the Kabbalist, empty space is not empty at all; it is suffused with fluctuating fields of energy which program the behavioral patterns of celestial bodies.

The three upper planets represent the enormous positive energy made available for use by mankind. The *Kriat Shema* prayer[13] considered by the Israelites to be the most powerful channel for this awesome power consists of two hundred and forty-eight words. This meditative channel provides energy-intelligence to the two hundred forty-eight bone segments of the human body.[14]

Bones do more than allow us to stand or walk. The marrow inside certain bones produces red blood cells that carry oxygen and nutrients throughout the body. The marrow in other bones makes millions of white cells that destroy harmful bacteria. The idea of infusing our bone structure with the awesome power from the cosmos takes on an even greater significance.

Consequently, our three distant planets act differently and independently from their seven sister planets. They do not perform the task of cosmically influencing our universe. Rather, their purpose out there is to contain the awesome power of the Force to be drawn upon by those who properly know and understand their function. Therefore, the Kabbalists do not include these three planets in their discussion of astral influences.

While everyone agrees with some statements about the universe, there is disagreement about most concepts concerning the cosmos. And when the Kabbalist provides precise information regarding our distant celestial bodies, there is no doubt that scientists unanimously will scoff at their findings.

However, let us remember that the details of scientific theoretical understanding are not completely certain and their experimental verifications of the theory are sparse if not nonexistent. Kabbalists have a good idea about what is happening out there. Their precise description of the Sun and its family makes one wonder how they arrived at their conclusions. Did they possess some type of spacecraft that permitted landings on these celestial bodies?

As explained in *Power of Aleph Beth*[15], the Kabbalist possessed the software to travel back in time and touch base with the beginnings and origin of celestial bodies. Thus their command of and knowledge about these entities did not require any flight into the uncharted terrain of space. Their extraterrestrial connection was and is established right here within the terrestrial realm.

Let us now return to a further clarification of our three outermost planets. As previously stated, the three essential elements are water, fire and air. Water, considered the positive physical expression of the Force, is known by its sfirotic code name *Hokhmah*.[16] Thus Pluto, expresses the all-inclusive positive energy-intelligence of the Force and makes its journey around the Sun in two hundred and forty-eight years. Neptune expresses the fire element of the Force, known by its sfirotic code name *Binah*,[17] and makes its journey around the Sun in one hundred sixty-four years, twice the time it takes Uranus to make the same journey. Uranus, expressing the air element of the Force, is known by its sfirotic code name of *Da'at*[18] and this planet takes only eighty-four years to complete its journey around the Sun.[19]

The idea just presented as to "why" each planet rotates in the time it does around the Sun can be understood by referring to Rabbi Isaac Luria's explanation concerning the various formations of the human head.

Why are there four colors in the eye (white, red, the different color for each person, and the color black for the pupil)? Why are there three chambers in the ears? Why two nostrils in the nose? And why one chamber for the mouth?

It is not our purpose to confuse the reader. The highly complex language of Kabbalah evolved slowly over a millennium in response to the ever-widening, deepening knowledge of the nature of man's intimate relationship with the cosmos. It continues to develop, expand, and ripen to this day.

The Kabbalist's task is, by no means, an easy one: using illusionary symbols, he attempts to provide a reasonable explanation for that which is beyond reason, to give expression to that which cannot be expressed, to illuminate concepts that are beyond the range of the senses. And, as if that were not enough, he must do all this with words that already have other fixed connotations and denotations that are often the antithesis of the concepts he is trying to express.

Is it any wonder that not everyone can understand what the Kabbalist has to say? The language of Kabbalah is of necessity a finite and therefore limited expression. But the concepts of Kabbalah, the indelible truths, can be comprehended by those who read with their hearts and not just with their eyes, and who listen with their minds and not just their ears.

The reader should be reminded that while Rabbi Isaac Luria was imparting to his disciples the Kabbalistic interpretation of the beginnings of Creation, each and every point mentioned had practical application here on the physical plane of existence. The process of the four stages discussed in such great detail by Rabbi Luria is much more than just the process through which the universe came into being. It is the process through which everything emerges from the primordial "stew" of Creation into physical, conceptual or even theoretical being.

The Ari was discussing the four phases or stages through which anything and everything must pass so as to become manifested. That process *never* changes. Whether we are discussing the birth of a child, the growth of a tree, the movement of tides or quantum tendencies, the process remains the same. The outer manifestations may differ radically, but not the internal process of the four emanations.

The laws of cause and effect — which are equally valid in the metaphysical world — dictate that the process proceed step by step through the four phases. And while to the casual observer this part of Kabbalah may seem complex, by observing the world through the framework of the four phases, all things become intelligible. Instead of getting lost in the millions of outer manifestations, the Kabbalist, by observing but a single process, can understand all things.

In the four phase process, the first phase contains and is inclusive of all subsequent phases. The root of a tree contains its own energy-intelligence and of those that evolve and follow. The trunk, branch and fruit are all contained — albeit not physically expressed — within the root. Consequently, the root essentially contains four energy-intelligences. The trunk will contain only three energy-intelligences; its own and the subsequent two energy-intelligences that emerge and so on until the emergence of the fruit which contains its own final energy-intelligence concluding the evolutionary process.[20]

The identical evolutionary process applies to the internal energy-intelligences of the human head. The eyes, considered by the Ari as the coded energy-intelligence of *Hokhmah* contains four energy-intelligences: its own, and that of the ears, nose and mouth. Therefore the eyes contain four colors, each indicating a specific energy-intelligence. The ears represent phase two of the evolutionary process of the head as the coded energy-intelligence of *Binah* and includes within its domain three energy-intelligences, its own, and that of the nose and mouth. Consequently, the ears contain three chambers, each specifying an energy-intelligence. The nose, the coded energy-intelligence of *Zeir Anpin* within the evolutionary process, consists of and encompasses two energy-intelligences and therefore has two nostrils. The mouth, known by its coded energy-intelligence of *Malkhut* has only its own energy and therefore contains only one aspect, one chamber.

Consequently, the Ari's revelation of an "inclusiveness" in any evolutionary process provides us with a striking clarification as to why the three outermost planets journey around the Sun in the time they do. Pluto, as *Ḥokhmah*, contains its own energy-intelligence that propels its orbit of 248 years. Pluto contains the other two manifested energy-intelligences of the Force, namely, Neptune and Uranus. Neptune as the coded energy-intelligence of *Binah*, or the fire element, journeys 164 years around the Sun; Uranus, which manifests the element of air and coded energy-intelligence of *Da'at* rotates approximately 84 years around the Sun; thus, the combined orbits of Neptune and Uranus amount to 248 years.

Kabbalistic astrology relates to the number seven; seven celestial bodies that poise their astral influences on earth as physically expressed by the seven planets known as Saturn, Jupiter, Mars, Sun, Venus, Mercury and Moon. Their internal energy-intelligence originates and stems from the seven encapsulated packets of energy known as the seven *Sfirot*[21].

These seven packets of energy also become expressed as motivating forces that empower the symmetry by which the external senses, namely, sight, sound, smell and taste become manifested. Each packet governs the two eyes, two ears, two nostrils and the mouth. These energy centers filter down from the original Light force throughout the astral bodies and finally express themselves as our senses[22].

The Kabbalistic interpretation and understanding of our senses thus provide us with a valid comprehension as to why our senses are different in each human being. There are no two people who have come into this world at the precise same moment. If by some unlikely chance this did occur, then indeed, the senses of these two individuals would be exactly alike.

Consequently, if, one day, mankind awakes from its sleep and asks who gave thought to, and where did the idea of seven days in a week come from, the answer from Kabbalah will be awaiting all those who seek to know. And for those who seem satisfied with the belief that a few thousand years ago a Creator set aside six days, and in that time made the world and every kind of animal and plant in it, just as is written in Genesis and rested on the seventh day, the question that must be raised is "why couldn't the Creator create everything in one day or ten days?"

There are many questions that science cannot confidently answer on the basis of theory and experiment. The scientist can only speculate as we all can. Of all the Biblical concepts, none is more central to the idea of Genesis than the concept of the days of the week. The facts as they exist today testify that the Biblical contention that a week consists of seven rotations of the earth is the considered calculation in our daily lives. Throughout the globe man considers a week's span of time in terms of seven days.

However, the Biblical version of the Creation of the universe in seven days is vague concerning what exactly transpired. The Zohar repeatedly states that the entire Bible is a cosmic code. From seemingly insignificant Biblical tales emerge the Zoharic and hence Kabbalistic interpretation of Creation.

It is the intention of this book to see back to the beginnings of the universe. All intelligent energies must, of necessity, have been included within the vast scope of the "Endless." They then became physically expressed through the senses, through rotations of the earth and other manifested states which are expressed in terms of seven.

The *Sefer Yetzirah* or *Book of Formation*, distinguished by its brevity, represents a theoretical approach to the problems and answers of cosmology and cosmogony. Even the most comprehensive of the numerous editions do not exceed seventeen hundred words.

Historically, this work is the earliest existing text written in the Hebrew language. Its chief subject matters are the elements of the entire cosmos and its occupants — the master code or DNA of all Creation. The twenty-two letters of the Hebrew *Aleph Beth* together exhibit the mysterious forces whose convergence produces the various combinations observable throughout the whole of Creation.

I began by making the claim that Kabbalah offers a precise path in the search to provide answers for longstanding scientific questions. Unlike science which is concerned solely with the *how* of things, Kabbalah is concerned with the *why*. It is my deep conviction that only by understanding the root factors of our universe and its natural laws can we begin to comprehend their meaning. Whatever road we take, our *fate* is indissolubly bound up with the internal forces of extraterrestrial bodies. Thus, it is essential for us to return to the source of these intelligent energies.

With all the interest and research efforts of the scientific community directed at the cosmos, science is still light-years away from appreciating the human link between heaven and earth. The Kabbalistic world view, on the other hand, provides another and refreshing approach to illuminating the cosmic darkness. The central life-force entities of the universe were created through the energy-intelligences which have come to be represented by the code name called *Sfirot*. These in turn have been channeled by the letters of the Hebrew *Aleph Beth*.

The elements of water, fire and air come into being by virtue of the three upper *Sfirot: Hokhmah, Binah* and *Da'at*. The seven planets in the world, seven days in a week, seven gates or openings of the senses in man, were created by the seven coded *Sfirot* of *Hesed* (Mercy), *Gvurah* (Judgment), *Tiferet* (Beauty), *NetzaH* (Victory), *Hod* (Splendor), *Yesod* (Foundation) and *Malkhut* (Kingdom).

The twelve signs of the Zodiac which established the twelve months in the year and twelve basic parts of the body were brought about by a combination of the coded *Sfirot* that brought about the seven planets.[23]

The decision by the monthly planners to establish a twelve month calendar is understandable even without having a clue to its real significance. The average person is aware that the calendar is structured around orbital flights by the earth around the sun. A thin belt of stars stretches across the sky against which the earth and moon can be seen to travel. They pass through twelve constellations which are stars that form the actual outlines of the twelve signs. Mathematically, the Zodiac is divided into twelve segments, or signs, at 30 degrees of arc. The twelve arcs correspond to the twelve constellations.

Therefore, from a very pragmatic point of view, it appears self-explanatory that a calendar be comprised of twelve months and consequently not necessarily linked to twelve astral influences. The days of the week present another problem. Why not simply count the days of the week from day one to day thirty or thirty-one and forget the notion of a seven-day week?

Early Kabbalists were familiar with the internal cosmic fields of celestial bodies and regarded each constellation and planet as an intelligent entity. Their observations of the universe, drawn from the various source reflections of the Zohar, enabled them to provide a valid guide for the individual in his search for total understanding.

With this in mind, let us return to our question as to *why* seven days? The Kabbalist viewed the seven days as intelligent entities motivated by internal energies, the seven *Sfirot*, which manifest as the seven days of the week. Consequently, mankind, consciously or otherwise, understood an intrinsic seven-day cycle, each portraying a peculiar energy-intelligence. And with the passing of the seventh day, the energy-intelligence of Sunday made its presence and influence felt again. The eighth day was not merely another complete rotation of the earth from darkness to light again. Rather, their keen perception and sensitivity experienced the same character of an energy-intelligence that they felt seven days earlier.[24]

Each day reflected a particular display of sfirotic energy-intelligence, although the forces that dictate man-inspired events remain largely unseen and unknown. While a fixed position is placed upon every individual, there are choices one can make by which the elements of distress can be removed. It is therefore essential that mankind become familiar with the forces that perhaps regulate his every decision and movement.

In conclusion, the Bible, according to Kabbalistic wisdom, is a cosmic code that must be deciphered. With a Zoharic perspective of Biblical Creation, the *whole* of Genesis takes on new meaning. Each day of Creation reveals a new dimension, or framework of energy-intelligence.

The ongoing conflict between the foes of evolution and those who believe in biological evolution continue to ignore the Kabbalistic doctrine that the Biblical story of Creation is an idea not to be taken literally. Furthermore, the concept of the Bible as history also misses the mark. The fact is that the Bible is more concerned with providing mankind with the tools to enhance our personal well-being than with presenting some tales, narrations or history.

The Force reveals itself in a myriad of patterns which

stem from relatively few archetypal designs. By connecting with the Force we assure ourselves of certainty; with control over the planets we tap the awesome power of the cosmos.

Knowledge is the connection, the planets are the channels. Let us now begin our journey into planetary exploration.

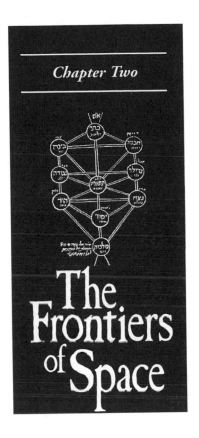

Chapter Two

The Frontiers of Space

EACH TIME ANOTHER ASTRONOMY RESEARCH SATELLITE goes up, a river of data comes streaming down. Astronomers now consider this flood of information a mixed blessing. As data has piled up, they have had to deal with a mass of facts that confuse rather than inform.

Astronomically speaking, the shell of air that encloses the earth is nothing but, to use a metaphor, a wet blanket. It ruins what would otherwise be a terrific view of the universe. To complicate matters, the wind consistently reshapes the contours and thickness of atmospheric layers, and this causes unpredictable viewing conditions. Fuzzy images and mirages are usually the result of telescopic readings.

Every scientific experiment is conditional on the part of

the observer and limited by the tools available for the analysis. The data available from incredibly distant galaxies are conditioned by how light reacts in our own experience. As we probe farther and farther into space, we are no longer looking at the universe as it is, but rather as it was when the light we see began its travel. We can no longer be certain that the star which sent the light even still exists.

Perhaps this might be the underlying reason why astronomers are often the most vociferous attackers of astrology. They are possibly aware of the slender threads upon which their theories have been formulated and conclusions based. What is more frustrating for the scientist is the realization that most if not all of their celestial theories contribute little to the conduct of or support in our daily lives. They neither resolve nor assist us in the removal of humankind traumas and difficulties.

Except for the accomplishment of the astronauts' landing on the Moon, there has been very little value, if any, added for Earth to become a better place to live in. Astrology provides a picture of the person's internal reality. We can understand the needs and motivating factors of individuals.

In our discussion of Saturn and the other planetary bodies, we shall become acquainted with a precise surface description of these celestial bodies. This information is readily available by the Kabbalist for all who seek its knowledge. Unfortunately astronomers, pursuing their endeavors with tunnel vision, are thereby denied the opportunity to access into the awesome power and knowledge of our universe and its collection of celestial players.

Saturn and its sister planets represent life urges channeled through them by our predetermined incarnated cassettes we established in a prior lifetime or lifetimes. They are, therefore, considered the stimuli in any given area of life. Planets and signs represent the paths in which the basic human urges and needs are likely to be expressed. They are screens or filters of what enters as our robotic-consciousness.

Oblivious to their stimuli, a person becomes a slave to their influences. An informed participant in the cosmic scenario provides free will and mastery over one's destiny. Given the nature of the problem or the plans an individual may have, one can then achieve an excellent perspective and understanding of why things happen the way they do and act accordingly.

Let us therefore begin our cosmic journey into the frontiers of space and rendezvous with our first celestial companion, albeit, the most distant one. However, before we begin our trip into the *control tower* of our cosmos, one point must be reiterated. There is no way that we can achieve any measure of influence or even supremacy over the celestial realm without *complete* knowledge of their composition and nature.

This applies to our own everyday evaluations and judgments. A physician cannot properly diagnose a patient without a comprehensive picture of the patient's character, nature and habits. No business venture or undertaking can achieve any measure of success without a proper evaluation and knowledge of all the factors involved. No marriage can be crowned with success without a prior commitment to the awareness of each other's nature, habits and characteristics.

Thus, the Kabbalist has gone to great lengths to provide all of mankind with as complete a description of our celestial realm as they deemed necessary to accomplish dominion over our space companions. Without this sort of control, there is *absolutely* no hope that we can arrange our affairs effectively on planet Earth.

Furthermore, pursuing an attitude of self-reliance in which the only factor to be reckoned with is *my* ability to succeed, *my* wisdom that is the determining cause for success or failure, is a folly proven by experience. "The best laid plans of mice and men go oft astray."

Consequently, a "new order of thought" must pervade the thinking of all mankind. Firstly, we must begin to question the "why" of anything and pursue our investigation until we have reached a satisfactory explanation. The reservoir of Kabbalistic teaching and knowledge can provide the necessary answers to any and all of our "whys." Secondly, we must surrender our egocentricity to the Lightforce with the firm conviction that our own capacities are limited and need the support of the Lightforce.

Only by means of a comprehensive road map can we even hope to achieve some form of stability and certainty in our lives. That road map of life's journey is the Bible as interpreted by the Kabbalah, without which dark areas along our path will cause us to stumble, fall and at times never recover.

Knowledge is crucial, for knowledge is the connection. What one does not "know" is that with which one has not come in contact. "Adam *knew* Eve and she conceived and bore Cain."[25] How can the mere act of knowing create a pregnancy? The Zohar explains this simply as the difference between information and knowing.

Knowing is the connection. Obviously, there was an act of physical intercourse. The point the Zohar makes in citing the particular verse in Genesis is to illustrate that the only time we

can make contact with something is when we have absorbed knowledge. Without knowledge there is no connection.

Once we meet these two requirements, then assuredly we have taken a quantum leap forward into a new dimension, the uncharted frontier of space. The unfamiliar realm of our celestial systems constitute the timeless, spaceless domain we must reach and make contact with if we are to be true masters of our destiny. For all the inviolability of the basic destiny pattern, we do have a degree of freedom almost without limitation to determine the life processes that unfold in the present lifetime.

Then, and then only, can we truly be liberated from the pattern of destiny that seems so unalterable and come to grips with our problems. A commitment to self-knowledge and self improvement is the first requirement of any individual who wishes to take control of his life and alter his destiny. Once that commitment is made, the results can be immediate and fulfilling.

Suddenly one notices that much of the confusion and discouragement that appeared so overwhelming gradually begins to disappear. This phenomenon will come about because of this commitment and the subsequent improvement in the quality of our daily existence.

While the individual is born into certain circumstances about which he has absolutely no say — his parents, ancestry, social standing or physical and mental characteristics — he can, as we have discussed, take control of his life and change his astrological chart.

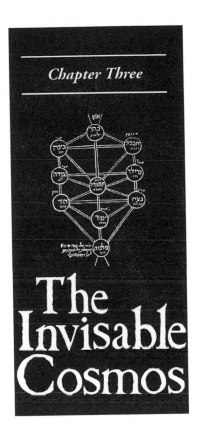

Chapter Three

The Invisable Cosmos

WHEN WE GET DOWN TO MATTERS BEYOND OUR immediate experience, the concept of "out there" and "really there" and so on begins to lose its significance and relevance. Quantum mechanics seems to say the entities of the subatomic world cannot be pinpointed. Some even go so far as to theorize and suggest that they exist in a maze of random possibilities awaiting to be materialized in a particular way in some peculiar circumstance.

Does this suggest that the properties of matter are subject to, and created by the consciousness of human beings? According to many quantum physicists, when faced with the dilemma as to when an atomic object behaves like a wave and when it behaves like a particle, their answer seems to come right out of some science fiction comic strip. The answer, say these physicists, depends on whether the object is *observed.*

Unobserved, the atomic object appears as a wave spread over space. However, the instant it is observed the wave collapses to a point and behaves like a particle. Incredible as this assumption may sound, nevertheless, scientists are confident that the action of simple observation causes a wave to collapse and thus produce a particle.

For many of my readers including myself, the concept of "wave" or "particle" is sufficiently difficult to grasp. After all, we are not scientists. But when physicists begin to stretch their idea to the point where our observation of the atomic object and its activity alters its structure, that, in the opinion of most of us, is just taking the concept too far.

But according to Danish physicist Neils Bohr, the world of the atom is *fuzzy* and *obscure.* The atom only sharpens into concrete reality when it is observed. In the absence of any observation the atom is a ghost. It only actualizes when you look at it. In Heisenberg's celebrated uncertainty principle it says you *can't* know where an atom or its parts are located and also know *how* it is moving at one and the same time.

The idea of an atom with a definite location and motion is meaningless. Position and motion form two mutually incompatible aspects of the same reality. Upon *whom* does the decision rest whether to look for the "thing," the atom, or to look for its movement. Upon ourselves! Nevertheless, we are told by physicists that we cannot have both. When you want to focus onto the atom for its location, do not expect anything more than its place. When you seek its motion you find an atom with a speed and *not* location.

If all of this sounds confusing to us, and if all this sounds too mind-boggling to accept, we are not alone. Einstein and all other scientists will agree with us. But we may ask of ourselves, doesn't the world out there really exist whether we observe it or not? Does everything that happens out there do so for its own reasons or is it because it is being *watched* or observed by me? Our observations might reveal the atomic realm of reality, but do we *create* it just by looking and focusing on it?

We certainly have difficulty in trying to establish some clarity concerning atomic behavior, but isn't that due to our *own* inability and bungling when we decide to probe its nebulous domain? Though few professional physicists stop to think about the incredible philosophical meanings of quantum mechanics, the bizarre implications become evidenced immediately after their recognition.

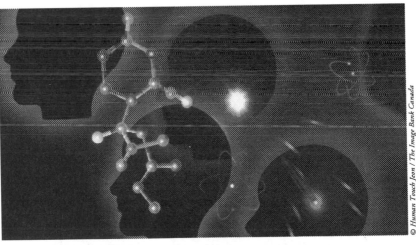

© Human Touch Jeon / The Image Bank Canada

And what seems to emerge is the convincing evidence that consciousness — the observer — plays a vital role in the nature of the physical, illusionary realm of reality.

Considering that the quantum theory has been with us

for a long time, it seems odd and truly remarkable that this incredible idea of the role played by man's consciousness on his environment has not filtered down to us, the layman. One might almost be led to believe that a secret conspiracy exists among physicists to retain a cloak of secrecy around their findings.

The idea that the scientific community considers the average layman incapable of comprehending their conclusion that atomic uncertainty is truly intrinsic to nature smacks of arrogance and intolerance. I would suspect that so long as nature's confusion is restricted to the subatomic world of existence, most of us feel only slightly uneasy that the world out there as we observe it is illusionary. After all, in daily life, the table and chair still remain a table and chair despite the *uncertainty* of their existence.

This is precisely the point the Kabbalist maintains when he stretches the notion of uncertainty even with respect to the table and chair. Simply because our 4% logical ability, and our severely limited vision — plus we'll throw in our ego for good measure — determine that the table is a table and the chair is a chair does not prove conclusively their physical reality and existence.

This is the heart of the question. Physicists, for all their faith and belief in the quantum theory, cannot come to grips with the glaring, physical world out there. Quantum says maybe it does not exist at all, and yet our five senses take over and declare, *hogwash*. Of course the chair is out there, and you must be crazy even to think of the chair as being illusionary. Facing the paradoxical nature of the physical reality has proved a harrowing experience for both physicists and mathematicians.

But, then again, what are chairs made of if not atoms.

How can lots of misbehaved, unpredictable, ghostlike things called atoms gather together to make something real and solid like the chair? The common sense view of the world—including the chair—in terms of things that really exist out there independent of our observation of its existence, completely breaks down in the face of the quantum factor.

Consequently, the chair may be a chair and then again maybe it's not. The atoms that make up 99% of the chair may be *particles* which explains for us why the chair is solid matter and why it is suitable for us to sit on it. However, if the atom is like a wave, not a wave of any substance or physical material, but rather a wave of information or knowledge, then the chair *is not there* until our knowledge determines that it is there.

The quantum factor has already determined for us that *nothing*, and I mean *absolutely nothing*, exists out there which can be independent of our observation, consciousness and thinking. And if my mind *wanders* like a *wave* and doesn't focus or concentrate on seeing the chair, then the chair for me does not exist.

This idea of a wandering mind is not so far out. How often have we been in a conversation with someone and suddenly our mind goes blank? In fact, we may be told by the other person that he observed our face or eyes and exclaims, "you look spaced or blanked out." Or, when one wanders through a memory file for a word or incident and does not achieve a recall, the expression for this failure is "I drew a blank."

Another example of a quantum dilemma is the notion known as background-figure illusions. These figures seem to portray radically different pictures depending on what aspects of the picture the eye chooses to view as background rather than the figure. The

most celebrated one of these illusions is known as the reversible goblet. If the viewer treats the black regions in the picture as background, he sees a white goblet against a black background. In contrast however, if the white area is treated as the background and the black region as figure, then one sees the profiles of two faces looking at each other.

Strange as it may seem, no one ever sees *both* pictures in a background-figure illusion at the same time. Psychiatrists interpret this phenomenon as reflecting a fundamental limitation of the mind's ability to process visual information. This sort of conclusion is an example typical of all medical interpretation when there is no conclusive evidence to support their findings.

However, if we were to take this illusionary paradox one step further, we come to realize that our problem with the background-figure illusion runs much deeper than merely a limitation of the mind's ability to process visual information. Apart from the mental reservation of viewing two aspects at the *same time*, we also come to realize the lack of control of the conscious mind.

One may *intend* to observe one of the two aspects. The eyes however, wander back and forth between the two aspects with little or no control of the conscious mind. Despite all concerted and concentrated efforts, we usually lose our focus on the one aspect and wander on to the next aspect.

Typically we assume that our lives, actions and thoughts are subject to our conscious mind control, should we decide to exert it. Yet, most researchers now agree that the unconscious process plays the vital role in virtually every phase of the brain's operational procedures and functions. This unconscious process significantly determines and molds what we *observe*, what we think, and how we interpret and respond to the world outside of ourselves.

In *To the Power of One*, I describe the emerging view of thought consciousness and its implications. The mistaken illusion is that we still cling to the notion that *we* dictate the direction and scope of our awareness. The fact is that the mind is arranged by metaphysical unseen forces to function so as to present us with a constructed and structured reality which we become conscious or aware of and subsequently experience in its final, completed version.

That which we perceive and sense in the conscious mind is the product completed for us just beyond the twilight zone of awareness. The material of awareness has come to us from the realm of the brain that can *scan*, *select* and *sort* out the array of quanta information available from present and past experiences. How long can or does this process take? Within the intangible and metaphysical realm of our mind, fractions of seconds have no meaning. This process takes place beyond any concept of time. No computer, regardless of its high-tech ability, can even match the thoroughness or speed of a human, mental computer.

The newly emerging cognitive models of the brain are compared to the way computers process information. They describe the mind as the software that directs the flow of data through our brain which is compared to the hardware. However, what is noteworthy about these new models is the agreement that the consciousness is treated as a later stage occurring outside the realm of the unconscious.

The clear message from the above appears to be that we cannot take *any physical behavior* into account without considering the conscious, brain experience. And more importantly, we cannot fully comprehend the conscious experience without re-cognizing the importance and input of the unconscious metaphysical processes. What seems to emerge from most recent studies is that we cannot ignore the concept of unconscious metaphysical processes.

What is noteworthy about the new cognitive models is how little influence our conscious mind exerts over our physical senses and behavior. Little wonder then that what we think may not really be the thought of a conscious mind, and what we observe may not be the observation we believe we saw. Thus, the conscious mind does not play the dominant or key role we once thought it did. Then it follows logically, that our observations are of such limited quality and ability that it seems foolish to place much emphasis or credibility on their conclusions.

If all of the aforementioned seems to be pervasive in the scientific community, then why does science continue its exercise in futility down a path that must end with inconclusiveness. In fact, to read much of the new scientific, so called, discoveries in newspapers and scientific journals one becomes appalled when reaching the final sentence of these articles. Almost without exception it concludes with "of course these findings still remain inconclusive, unsupported by hard evidence."

One then must throw the entire research and development program into question. If the naked eye, our conscious thought, is part of an illusionary realm, then why do we pursue further research by physical application when these devices are inconclusive support to their theories and hypotheses?

We now have billion dollar copper coils of particle accelerators and atom smashers in which atoms are smashed together.

Billions of dollars, francs, pounds and marks are being spent to look into the very heart of the atom. Physicists are learning the innermost secrets of matter (so we are told) and the energy that holds all things together. When they are all finished, instead of being awed by this display of technology, we should be appalled. All this money, all these machines and what does it do for us, the people?

The purpose of this chapter in particular and the book in general is not to criticize ongoing scientific research. Rather, it is about the impact of their findings, which of necessity has produced for us the uncertainty principle. I make no attempt to discuss in detail their findings. This is a chapter about human consciousness and its severe limitations.

The reader should not be deterred by the technical jargon. This chapter is primarily intended to arouse an awareness of consciousness for the general reader with no previous knowledge of science. I do not believe that some of the recent work on cosmology, mind/brain/consciousness has previously come to the attention of the layman.

Towards the end of this chapter tentative answers to the scientific dilemma begin to emerge—answers based on the Kabbalistic conception of nature and its reality. The answers may not be totally satisfying, but I believe the Kabbalist is uniquely placed to provide them. It may seem bizarre but, in my opinion, Kabbalah offers the *only* path to a quantum understanding of the uncertainties quantum mechanics has raised in this century.

Furthermore, the simplicity with which the Kabbalist explains away the complexities of our universe could now be within the grasp of the layman. When physicists provide a *loophole* to the age-old assumption that "one cannot get something for nothing," they have begun to tamper with the human fabric of decency. To attribute this astonishing presumption to some spectacular recent advances in physical science, even if these assumptions represent the very foundation of the New Age of Physics and the Quantum Theory, is a betrayal of the trust placed in science by the lay people.

For the Uncertainty Principle and other scientific conclusions — which may be totally wrong — to become the bedrock of a "free universe" concept undermines the pillars of our civilization. With their uncertainty which they readily admit to, they attempt to remove the one idea mankind has for so long clung to, namely responsibility and accountability.

With so much of physics riding on uncertainty and illusion one might have imagined that science would "throw in the towel" admit to its demise and start all over again. Whatever the outcome of scientific endeavor and the infinite waste that surrounds these luxurious, public-relations minded projects, the truth concerning the universe shall ultimately reign supreme.

Werner Heisenberg, the famous physicist and father of the Uncertainty Principle, stated at the end of his paper in the Zeitschrift, "We *cannot* know, as a matter of principle, the present (now) in all its details." This is where quantum theory cuts free from the determinacy of classical ideas. For what quantum mechanics says is that *nothing* is real and that we cannot say anything about what things are doing when we are not looking at them.

The laws of physics that we are familiar with in the everyday world no longer work. Einstein, and many other scientists, found it incomprehensible, and refused to accept all of the implications of the theory. The idea was anathema to Einstein. "The

Lord does not play dice," he said, referring to the theory that the world is governed by the accumulation of outcomes of essentially "random choices" of possibilities at the quantum level.

Einstein, as the Kabbalists before him, assumed there must be some underlying clockwork that makes for a genuine fundamental reality of things. The search for quantum reality has proved fruitless, since there is *no reality* in the everyday sense of the word. The scientists of today have been even more horrified than Einstein with the answers that we now have to the questions that keep cropping up.

Whatever the new idea concerning the reality of our universe, be it supergravity, parallel universes, expanding universe and many more, they are all accompanied by the same essential fiber that weaves through the fabric of each theory, *inconclusive and uncertain*. Whether it be the Nobel Prize Laureates with the super public relations personnel or minor, unknown scientists, the result is always the same.

When Sheldon Glaskow of Harvard University, Abdus Salam at Imperial College in London or Steven Weinberg of Harvard developed theories on symmetry, they shared the Nobel Prize in Physics for it in 1979, even though there was then *no* direct experimental proof that their idea was *even correct.*

The Kabbalist finds himself at odds with the idea that the behavior of atoms — and hence the entire universe — is governed by purely random physical processes. The Kabbalist claims there is an underlying order in the universe.

Future scientific research will thus have to be prepared for surprises that may come from the field of experience of nuclear physics as well as from that of cosmology. The path so far traced by the quantum theory indicates that an understanding of those still unclarified features of atomic physics can only be acquired by foregoing visualization and objectification to a greater extent than at present. One day abstract atomic physics will fit more harmoniously into the Kabbalistic world view of reality.

Thus, the uncertainty principle defines for us a technical barrier to obtaining the precise information necessary concerning momentum and position. Without this information we lack the critical precondition of all causal explanation in physics and other related matters. Neils Bohr and Werner Heisenberg believed that physics must pass over and ignore what it cannot define by experiment.

Understood by the traditional criteria of science, quantum theory was, indeed, fatally flawed. It could not provide explanations about reality. Bohr held that science must accept the fact that undefinable concepts such as causality and objective reality have no place in atomic physics.

What could never permit me to accept this permanent barrier was that to apply a flawed theory to a flawless universe meant anchoring the human mind to the present set of physical concepts.

By removing their "scientific" blinders and allowing themselves to drink from the wellspring of Kabbalistic thought they will have accessed into a wide array of conceptual tools. Neils Bohr maintained that man can *never* free himself from common sense notions about the physical reality. Why? Because these concepts saturate our language. Ultimately the result of every experiment must be translated and communicated in a language with which we are all familiar.

Furthermore, these scientists maintain that, insofar as man's limited range of reason and logic is concerned, the notion of a quantum world out there just doesn't exist; the reason being that no language exists to describe the quantum world of existence.

The French geneticist, Francois Jacob, once said that the reason physics became the ruler of the pack was that physics was the first to have its own language. That language was mathematics; but then something happened. We discovered a world beyond the five senses and everything changed. The language of mathematics no longer was capable of addressing thought, meta physics or the unseen realm of reality. The principle of uncertainty prevails, and there is no longer a language to explain it.

This forces any decent theoretical physicist to let go of solid ground and learn to become a mystic. In this, the Kabbalistic view becomes the only logic. Though Kabbalah often deals with profound matters, it does so in a language that can be easily understood, a process which in itself contains an important lesson. The method of communicating knowledge of the Kabbalah points to one of its central teachings. The Divine or Metaphysical world of infinity can be transformed into the finite and limited language of man.

The instrument by which the quantum realm of reality becomes conceptualized is the cosmic blueprint of the universe, the Bible. For the Kabbalist, the stories and tales of the Bible are coded messages by which the metaphysical realm, decoded by the Kabbalah, becomes revealed. Its language is the *Aleph Beth*.

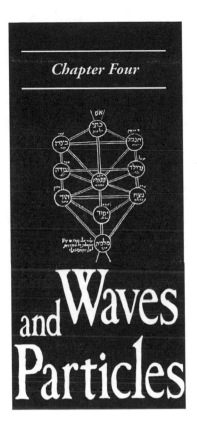

Chapter Four

and**Waves**
Particles

QUITE APART FROM THE SCIENTIFIC IMPORTANCE OF quantum theory to an understanding of the fabric of life, there are direct personal links between some of the leading characteristics in the quantum story of the particle-wave duality.

The basic equations of quantum theory lead to the uncertainty situation. However, when you start with uncertainty there is no way to work out the basic quantum equations. So we find ourselves in a catch 22 situation; the new quantum theory denies the idea of causality. This inability to make a determination was the first example of quantum weirdness. It implied the existence of physical events that were forever unknowable and unpredictable.

Another example of quantum confusion was that the

mathematics of quantum theory permitted both a particle-like and a wavelike representation for the electron. Is the electron a wave or a particle?

If you are finding this difficult, you are in good company; Neils Bohr, Werner Heisenberg and Wolfgang Pauli in Copenhagen, all Nobel Prize Laureates, debated these questions for over a year. In February, 1927, when *frustration* finally set in, they were all exhausted. They needed a break and went on vacation.

My purpose in discussing waves and particles and the quantum theory, is to draw our attention to the fact that physicists are just as confused as we are. Also, that Kabbalists do provide us with a description of the universe and all that it contains. In Kabbalah teachings there are no effects without cause. The wave/particle duality is not incomprehensible.

Simply explained, as described by Rabbi Isaac Luria, the duality of nature existed at the moment of Creation. There is an *urgent* need to understand the Kabbalistic concept of cause and effect. The Zohar recognized the futility of the investigative procedure which relies on observation to link cause and effect. The Zohar states that simply because we cannot visually observe and trace a cause to an effect, nor find it, does not imply the lack of a cause.

The primal cause of all terrestrial and celestial activity originates with the *actions of man*. Man's actions, even though they may be separated from their effects by time, space and motion, are not lost and forgotten.

The problem lies in man's inability to see the entire

scenario from beginning to end. However, this lack of control or incompetency must not provoke us into the hopelessness or helplessness that brought the aforementioned Nobel Laureates to their decision to accept the *Uncertainty Principle*. We must not abrogate or surrender our inalienable right to *know*. Einstein could never reconcile himself to the chance element that quantum theory took on.

He was distressed by the *indeterminacy* of the quantum theory. But that objection was not the main one that stood in the way of his accepting the theory's picture of reality. The intimate relationship of different systems that are not in spatial contact was a most fundamentally different and new feature. A principle of physics that he held even more dear than determinism was the principle of *local causality* — that distant remote events cannot instantaneously influence local objects without any mediation.

The finding, that there are intimate relationships even in systems that are not in spatial contact, frightened most physicists because they also held the principle of local causality sacred. What is the fundamental theory of local causality? Essentially it states that events far away cannot directly, and more importantly, instantaneously influence objects here.

An example of local causality is demonstrated by the following: If a fire breaks out one thousand miles away, there is no way it can directly influence you. What may happen is that a friend may call on the telephone immediately and tell you about the fire, but this is a simple causality. Information about the fire was transmitted by an observable electromagnetic signal. Local causality then is a term used to describe an observable, physical relationship between two points or between a cause and effect.

This was the principle which stood at the center of all our thinking in physics about our environment and matters that relate to our daily experiences. To accept a relationship between physical objects without an observable physical connection was unthinkable. The quantum theory, however, violates this principle of local causality.

As long as we thought in terms of *physicality* for the objective world, this setting sufficed as a starting point in resolving a host of problems, the consideration of which had occupied mankind for the previous two centuries. But quantum theory has upset the balance. The change in tone has been decisive.

At the start of the quantum principle or, as others phrase it, "the beginning of the *crisis* of atomic collapse" (illusionary from a Kabbalistic perspective) one conceived of the electron as headed on a deterministic path towards a point center of attraction. After the advent of quantum mechanics one learned to abandon the hope of explaining all phenomena as relations between objects existing in *space* and *time*. The ultimate ground for the failure of the principle of causality in subatomic physics, is the impossibility of describing subatomic processes in spatio-temporal terms that are adequate *only* for microscopic objects.

Werner Heisenberg[26] on this matter expressed it as follows:

> There exists a body of exact mathematical laws, but they cannot be interpreted as expressing simple relationships between objects existing in space and time. The observable predictions of this theory can be *approximately* described in

such terms, but not uniquely.

Consequently, recent developments in physical science have made evident the limitations of the theories of classical physics as universally adequate systems of explanation. These same developments have also brought under critical scrutiny the validity of many time-honored principles of scientific inquiry. Obviously, chief among these is the classical view that the aim of science is to discover the causal orders in which the events of nature occur.

Considering the limitations of classical physics, the search for causal orders is not likely to succeed. The objective of a universal science of physics whose laws and theories possess a strictly deterministic form must be cast as inherently unfulfilled.

Before proceeding to the Kabbalistic view of our universe, I deem it necessary to draw the reader's attention to the ideas and words of Max Planck, the discoverer of the quantum theory. If any man is to be credited with being the father of modern physics that man is Max Planck, winner of a Nobel Prize in 1918. Planck engraved his undisputed claim to it on December 14, 1900, when he announced his formulation of the *concept* that eventually became known as the quantum theory.

Planck was an individual whose approach to physics was of a high order because of his philosophical and ethical attitudes. He stated that[27] "conscientiousness and truth are the ideals that will lead the scientist along the true path, in life as in science. They will guarantee him, not necessarily brilliant results, but the highest good of humanity, namely, inward peace and true freedom."

If I did not know who Max Planck was, I would have mistaken him for a Kabbalist. Unfortunately, his beliefs and ideals do not necessarily pervade scientific research and endeavor. He was honest with his peers around him, but more important, he was honest with himself. I believe, and from what little I have read, know, that he practiced what he preached and discovered what only true Kabbalists find in their lives, *inner peace* and true freedom.

Conscientiousness and truth are just as necessary in the research in science as in one's personal practical life. Planck consistently pleaded for the researcher not to be blinded by any new intellectual discovery, nor to close one's eyes to results obtained from another point of view which may not necessarily fit in with one's own ideas. Furthermore, claimed Planck, causality is completely eclipsed by indeterminate probability, and the microcosm by the macrocosm.

Although he did believe that a fundamental unity and harmony existed in nature, he did not believe that the search for this underlying feature in nature would necessarily lead to mysticism. He considered it likely that new patterns of unity in nature will reveal themselves in the future.

Consequently, it should come as no surprise that with the present widespread interest and acceptance of Kabbalistic teachings, new patterns concerning the reality and unity of nature are surfacing. The unfolding and revealing of new ideas concerning our universe can be traced directly to the new, unforseen and unexpected discoveries presented by Rabbi Ashlag in his *Study of the Ten Luminous Emanations*. They are permeated with the spirit of metaphysics and mysticism, which follows the principles defined by Rabbi Isaac Luria, who arranged and collated the numerous individual observations and details which become part of one comprehensive picture.

The aim of this chapter is to achieve a total comprehension of the unity in nature as presented by the Kabbalist. The dilemmas facing the conscientious scientist are manifold. They include the idea of supposed collapse of the atom, and an indeterminate principle in our universe. Max Planck once wrote:

> There have been times when science and philosophy were alien, if not actually antagonistic to each other. These times have passed. Philosophers have realized that they have no right to dictate to scientists their aims and the methods for attaining them; and scientists have learned that the starting point of their investigation does not lie solely in the perceptions of the senses, and that science cannot exist without some small portion of metaphysics.
>
> Modern physics impresses us particularly with the truth of the old doctrine which teaches that there are realities existing apart from our sense-perceptions, and that there are problems and conflicts where these realities are of greater value for us than the richest treasures of the world of experience.[28]

At one time physics was solely concerned with the objects and events of inanimate nature. Twentieth century physics brought with it a new age, the awareness that water, fire, air, rocks and sand were made of active, vibrating atoms and molecules. Rabbi Ashlag stretched this revolutionary new perspective of our universe by including the element of *consciousness* into what were once considered by physicists as solely inanimate objects.

This startling revelation will explain away many of the anomalies that still plague twentieth century scientists, namely the quantum theory and its accompanying *Uncertainty Principle.* These New Age principles moved Einstein to write to a friend, "I cannot bear the thought that an electron exposed to a ray should by its own free decision choose the moment and the direction in which it wants to jump away. If so, I'd rather be a cobbler or even an employee in a gambling house than a physicist." He was disturbed by its claim that the objective physical world consists of basic building blocks, such as the electron and proton, whose individual actions *defy* the law of *cause* and effect.

Let us now begin our journey into the new and meaningful universe of Kabbalah. Our first step designated in the road map is Genesis, where it all began. No doubt, many of my readers would strongly disagree with my approach that with Genesis it all began. I need not refer here to the considerable number of religious dogmas to which physical science has dealt a fatal blow.

Genesis, and the Bible in general, was never meant to symbolize a form of religion. Rather, the entire Bible presents a quantum blueprint of our universe. The Bible, with its narrations, tales and commandments, according to the Zoharic interpretations, is a cosmic code waiting to be deciphered. It is to this task that the Kabbalah addresses itself.

There are many questions that science cannot confidently answer on the basis of theory and experiment. The scientist can only speculate — as we all can. If not science, where then do we begin our investigation into the question of why and how did life and the universe originate? Commonly, in the Western world, our initial exposure to this question is through the Biblical account of Genesis. A literal interpretation of Biblical Genesis is vague concerning what exactly transpired.

The Zohar is, for the uninitiated reader, decidedly abstruse. Fortunately, Rabbi Ashlag had the crucial insight to decipher certain portions of the Zohar which revealed the precise order in Creation and in the heavens. Consequently, from seemingly insignificant Biblical tales emerge the Zoharic and hence the Kabbalistic interpretation of the Big Bang.[29]

The problem of the ultimate origin of the physical universe and why it came about should lie within the boundary of science. Scientists have recently gone so far as to make serious attempts to understand how the universe may have appeared from nothing without violating any physical laws. The question that we must address is how can something come into existence without cause?

Quantum physics seemed to achieve this incredible phenomenon, inasmuch as quantum mechanics is intrinsically indeterministic and unpredictable. Existence without cause, effect without cause, runs contrary to the Kabbalistic view of our universe. This doctrine did not come about for religious, dogmatic reasons. As mentioned previously, this idea troubled Einstein and induced him to utter his famous words, "the Lord does not play dice with the universe."

For the Kabbalist, Einstein's response had no place within the lexicon of Kabbalah. When scientific experiments validated the conclusion that it is impossible to predict from one moment to the next how a quantum system will behave, objections by Einstein were ridiculed. Intuition and emotions cannot, nor do they, determine laws and principles of our universe.

Einstein made several attempts to re-establish the law of cause and effect, so solidly grounded in our daily experience. Within the world of quantum, spontaneous change is not only permitted, it is unavoidable.

The determinate and uncertainty principles were the only conclusions that physicists were left with when confronted with quanta phenomena. This led to the idea that it was no longer absurd to consider that the universe came into existence spontaneously from nothing, without cause.

For the Kabbalist, this notion is absurd. To believe that a daily newspaper came into existence spontaneously without cause is just as absurd as to consider that an entire complex universe turned up *without cause*.

The fact that scientists were ready to accept these ideas, albeit no other options were available, only led to other problems. From the Kabbalistic point of view, if there remain inexplicable phenomena, one should not take the escape hatch route and pray to the Lord that the problem disappear.

We should set aside our egocentricities and avoid finding refuge in some halfhearted notions. Scientists are still faced with the task of explaining by what physical processes the organized systems and complex activity that pervade the universe emerged from a Big Bang event.

The fact that the physical world around us has the ability to self-create and organize itself is a deeply mysterious property of the universe. The fact that we label this creative force as an aspect called *nature*, still does not provide us with an understanding as to the *nature* of this self-creating force.

Even the Big Bang theory which refers to a sudden explosion that triggered an ever-expanding universe fails to explain adequately how it expanded at just the right speed and with such amazing uniformity to create the galaxies, stars, the empty space, planets and other phenomena.

Some ascribe this phenomenon to the bizarre idea that all this came about at random, an idea that goes against the grain of Zoharic teaching. Others explain away this preposterous beginning and subsequent evolution as a Divine intervention.

Whatever the explanation, it does not, and should not convince any thinking individual. These ideas contradict the familiar physical surroundings we observe which suggest that things *do not* function in a random way. Why then are we to understand and accept bizarre ideas such as the *entire* universe emerging without cause. Atomic harmony and cosmic unity so elegantly displayed indicate a *thoughtful* universe.

When was the last time we read The New York Times while *all* of its employees were on strike? Has a farmer planting an apple seed witnessed a *self-creative* expansion of his initial effort — the seeding of his apple tree?

Most of us become awe-struck by the beauty and subtlety of nature. And yet, while some of us are inspired to believe that there must be a purpose behind existence, others consider the universe as utterly pointless. These latter scientists exercise a strong influence on prevailing thought. It should therefore, come as no surprise that human life has become so cheap. Considering the attitude of pointlessness, then what is the *point* of man's existence?

Isn't it strange that even on the largest scale of size, energy and matter are arranged in a non-random way? A glance at the evening sky reveals a powerful, awesome organization forming a meaningful group of energy-intelligence.

The idea of an expanding universe shows, from the very beginning, the insecurity of the astrophysicists along with their research. The uncertainty principle should have, once and for all, taken these scientists from the realm of egocentricity to one of humility. But, what did happen? They went deeper into their "desire to receive for the self alone". They came up with theories that defy and violate our surroundings, and stumble from one pitfall to another.

There is no such thing as an expanding universe. The eye is certainly not a dependable instrument of research. Many scientists believe that this century has seen an unprecedented expansion in our knowledge about the universe. This, they claim, is due largely to the powerful and precise instruments such as radio and optical telescopes.

Concepts such as the theories of relativity have overturned the long-dominant Newtonian Universe of absolute space and time. We have been forced to reconsider our notions about the universe. Unfortunately the relativity theory has changed our perception of the universe from an infinite and unchanging cosmos to a system thought to be a changing and expanding universe. This is Hubble's Law, which states that the Universe is expanding.

Then along came a Belgian astronomer George Lemaitre who made an attempt to explain the forces responsible for the dispersion of galaxies throughout space. He believed Hubble's expanding Universe was the remnant of a primordial explosion. Lemaitre thought that all matter had been concentrated originally in a super dense group, which exploded for *unknown reasons* and began the expansion of the cosmos.

And yet, Lemaitre's attempt to determine whether the universe will continue to expand without limit or eventually collapse and return to its original state was unsuccessful because even today the density of matter in space cannot be precisely measured.

The reader might, by this time, be wondering why I touch on intricate, scientific studies of our cosmos instead of proceeding directly to the point of Kabbalistic interpretation. The reason is, I want to acquaint the reader with as much scientific thinking about the cosmos as possible, thus, to understand where the Kabbalistic world view is coming from.

Also, due in part to the observational problems posed by the Big Bang model, the point that is being made is the inevitable inconclusiveness of *all* scientific cosmic research. Astronomers continue to speculate, when in fact Kabbalists have all along known the certainty of the universe. Whether the universe is expanding forever or ultimately collapsing and re-expanding continues to be hotly debated. Scientists can *imagine* innumerable laws which can serve any purpose, yet, without being able to state why one of them is to be preferred to the others.

Another subject that must be dealt with, before embarking on our Kabbalistic journey into space, is the subject of "missing matter." Physicists *believe* or suspect that a ghost, or missing matter, makes up 90 percent of the universe. It is a jarring thought that we cannot see most of the matter in the universe. This ghost or missing matter has become one of the biggest questions in science today.

Some scientists suggest that these invisible particles number 10,000 billion per cubic inch of space, a sum the brain will find difficulty in conceptualizing. The quantum theory predicts a remarkable symmetry in our universe, which should exist between matter and antimatter. Since it *appears* that matter dominates largely over antimatter, scientists have concluded that our world *does not* have this symmetry.

Physicists are happy about this since, if it were otherwise, the annihilation of matter caused by antimatter would mean the end of all massive particles. For this reason it is thought that all the stars, galaxies and dust we observe in the universe are in the form of matter rather than antimatter.

Antimatter, which still remains ghostlike, is identical to ordinary matter except that the signs of the electric charges of the particles making up antimatter are reversed. Scientists claim that large pieces of antimatter do not exist in our world because matter and antimatter, if brought together, annihilate each other.

Scientists have concluded that, when a particle encounters an antiparticle, or matter confronts antimatter, mutual annihilation must result. Consequently it's believed that it is *unlikely* that more than a tiny fraction of the universe is made of antimatter. Thus the scientist continues to reach conclusions on invalid premises. In fact he too believes these premises may prove groundless. When the physicist observes that a mixture is violently unstable, he is forgetting that his participation in the observation determined the violence. The Kabbalist draws no such conclusions. A Kabbalist observing the activity of matter and antimatter will recognize the mutually harmonious and unified state of existence between the two. Violence, annihilation, and chaos are the products of mankind in his most obstinate frame of mind.

Scientists have known for some time that matter is not permanent in nature. It can be created and also destroyed. Presently, if enough energy can be concentrated, new particles of matter will come into existence. Matter can be seen as a form of locked up energy. The proposition, that energy can be converted into matter implies, that our universe may have begun in a matter-less state, and that all matter we now observe was generated from a field of energy the Kabbalist refers to as consciousness.[30]

The problem of the origin of the cosmos is truly baffling. One can imagine examining the seed of a tree, and, upon seeing the tree itself, realize that the secret of this self-creative process lay hidden within the seed. The universe itself, however, does not furnish us with the seed or blueprint of our observable universe. The Zohar, and the Kabbalistic commentaries, do just that. They provide us with the answers as to the origin of cosmic life.[31]

Let us now turn to the comprehensive and yet simple view of our universe as taught by the Kabbalist.

A process, referred to in Kabbalah as "Restriction," brought about the creative process referred to by the Kabbalist as the emanation of the ten *essential* energy-intelligences. The Restriction, the Big Bang itself, is the process that resulted in the manifestation of thought energy-intelligence, the first form of existence. "Restriction" may be compared to the action of the filament of an electric bulb, which by restricting the flow of energy ("big bang" between the electric current and filament) produces a physically manifested expression of light. The final act first becomes manifest as thought consciousness.[32]

The Kabbalistic version of how the universe got started has already been fully discussed in most of my other publications.

Also, the essential purpose of this work is to provide a cosmic blueprint and roadmap with which we may enhance our daily lifestyle. Science is by no means any closer to unraveling the mysteries of our universe and how they affect our physical and mental well-being; perhaps because behind this physical enigma lies a deeper metaphysical mystery.

Physicists are not impervious to the magnetism of metaphysics. Einstein credited *intuition* as the principal factor in his discovery of the theory of relativity. He spent his remaining years searching for a simple, elegant formula by which to explain the nature of the universe within the framework of a single unified conceptual construct. Subsequent generations of scientists have taken up the gauntlet and the search for a Grand Unified Theory continues to this day. Is physics only *now* learning what metaphysics has known all along?

In these fragmented times, bombarded as we are by sensory stimuli, what perfect pleasure it gives one to enter the refuge of an ancient tradition that is at the same time so elemental and yet so complete. It is with eager anticipation that Kabbalists await scientific verification of a Grand Unified Theory. For not only will that announcement corroborate many metaphysical philosophies and doctrines, it will confirm what Kabbalists have known for centuries. Namely, that there is another *invisible*, all pervading energy-intelligence, not unlike gravity or electromagnetism, that has yet to be scientifically substantiated. And that every facet of this primal force field is in constant instantaneous communication with every other phase and facet. Ironically, science will be forced to accept and once again embrace those very selfsame spiritual, supernal, and supernatural doctrines and traditions that it struggles so arduously to discredit and destroy.

Kabbalah and science may have more in common than practitioners of either discipline would care to admit. Both, after all, seek to explain the true nature of existence.

The Zohar declares that an understanding of Genesis and the Garden of Eden will provide us with a full understanding of the cosmos. The popular interpretations of the Bible were condemned by the author of the *Zohar*, Rabbi Shimon bar Yoḥai. According to bar Yoḥai, rather than being a detailed *religious doctrine*, the Bible is actually a complete code of our cosmology.[33]

The Biblical account of Creation and its supportive interpretation by the Zohar provides all of mankind with a perfect and satisfactory communication system by which we can connect with the quantum world of reality. Only then can we begin the journey to achieve mastery over our destiny instead of leaving matters of concern to chance. The Bible speaks in code, the Kabbalah does the deciphering.

> And out of the ground the Lord made to grow
> every tree that is pleasant to the sight and good
> for food, the Tree of Life also in the midst of the

garden, and the Tree of Knowledge of Good and Evil.[34]

And the Lord commanded the man, saying: of every tree of the garden thou mayest freely eat, but of the Tree of Knowledge of Good and Evil, thou shalt not eat of it; for on the day that thou eatest thereof thou shalt surely die.[35]

Of all the passages in the Bible, these particular verses carry with them the entire idea of cosmic energy reality. It is by far the most profound, most ancient and most widely held concept in Kabbalah. These three passages reveal the whole system of cosmology. From them we can learn the very essence of our universe and the very essence of the astral influences that completely envelop and, unfortunately at times, control the destiny of man. They demand tremendous change in our present theories of the building blocks of our universe and concepts of the whole spectrum of cosmology.

The following Zohar[36] emphasizes the existence of parallel universes which is revealed in the Biblical description of Genesis.

OF ALL THE TREES OF THE GARDEN THOU SHALT SURELY EAT. This means that he was permitted to eat them *all together*, for, as we see [of all the trees] Abraham ate, Isaac and Jacob ate, and all the prophets ate and remained alive. This tree [of knowledge] however, was a tree of death, insofar that he who ate it by *itself* was bound to die, since he took poison. Hence it says *in the day that thou eatest thereof thou shalt surely die*, because thereby he would be separating the

shoots....The words *of the fruit of the Tree* sig-
nify the woman [female] of whom it is written
"Her feet go down to death, her steps take hold
of the nether world"[37]

This does not, however, imply, that these fruits are from
the evil side, without any holiness, because the Bible considers
her as fruit-bearing essence [self creating], for only on the side
of the Dark Lord is there decay and discontinuity. "For in that
day that you eat from it, assuredly you shall die." By *itself* she
represents the tree of death.

In one of its most mysterious sections — a chapter
avoided by most translators and commentators — the Zohar
explores the methodology of cosmic balance. The Zohar cautions the reader of the Bible not to be misled by its literal
expression. The Bible uses language to imply an internal cosmic
truth that is beyond the reach of the rational mind.

However, for the uninitiated reader the Zohar is decidedly abstruse. Fortunately, Rabbi Ashlag had the crucial insight
to decipher certain statements about the universe in the Zohar
which reveal the precise order in Creation and in the heavens.
Consequently, from seemingly insignificant Biblical tales
emerges the Zoharic, and hence Rabbi Ashlag's, Kabbalistic
interpretation of the structure of the universe.

The Zohar and other Kabbalistic treatises present views
in a manner similar to those of the physicists. The physicist presents theories in the language of physics, and basic Kabbalistic
treatises present knowledge in the language of metaphor and
symbolism. Both remain far and beyond the comprehension of
the reader. Science attempts to ascertain the truth about our
universe by methods acceptable to science. Kabbalah, on the

other hand, was provided with the truths about our universe at the very outset by the Bible, the Zohar, and the *Sefer Yetzirah*. The task now left for the Kabbalist, like Rabbi Ashlag, was to set down in comprehensive language the knowledge already presented in the aforesaid basic sources.

Consequently, the reader is requested to *maintain* the desire for a road map that provides signposts along the route of life's existence, and not to be troubled by the initial presentations of the Zohar. The purpose of entering these concealed and abstruse treatises of the Zohar is to establish direct contact with the source of our road map. They establish and provide for us a path to an elevated state of consciousness and awareness necessary to understand the subsequent interpretations in a simple, comprehensible language.

When the knowledge of Kabbalah is understood, its fantastic simplicity will be fully appreciated. The Zohar[38] states that, "in the days of Messiah, there will no longer be the necessity for one to request of his neighbor, teach me wisdom, as it is written,[39] ... and they shall teach no more every man his neighbor, and every man his brother, saying, Know the Lord; for they shall all know Me, from the least of them to the greatest of them."

The route to this frontier lies beyond the realm of the mathematical systems of quantum and the universe. These are but paving stones. The Kabbalah is the road itself. According to the Zohar, the day is nearing when the inner secrets of nature that have remained so long in hiding, will at last be revealed. Such knowledge will enable us to reach the very essence of that which is of us and around us.

It will permit us to access to the "non-space" domain.

It will provide us with a framework for the comprehension of not only our familiar observable universe, but also of that which lies beyond the range of observation in the realm of the metaphysical.

Quantum Theory demolished the view we once held that the universe sits "out there" while we are objective observers of what transpires in it, safely insulated from the action. Quantum mechanics has shown the observer and the observed to be as twiddle-dum and twiddle-dee. The observer has an incalculable impact on the electron and an unpredictable influence on its future.

To that degree, the course of the universe has been altered by human thought. In this way, we are led to a reconciliation of Quantum and Kabbalah since both maintain that this is a participatory universe.

Who is this observer-creator about whom we have spoken? He is man, the initiator of thought. "Sof Ma'seh B'makhshava Tehila," declares Rabbi Solomon Alkabetz, medieval author of the hallowed Sabbath hymn *"Lekha Dodi"* (Come, My Beloved). "All manifestations and actions are merely the results of *a priori* thought." The laws of cause and effect are valid in the metaphysical, non-observable realm just as they are in the material, physical world.

We have no trouble identifying that which is material. We can touch it. It has a body, substance. It is the cause of which the effect has been the evolution of all of our senses. We can see, smell, and hear it. But, when we get down into the substance of that which we perceive as solid, physical reality, we return to the basic building block of nature — the electron. And what is an electron? Is it a microscopic bit of solid matter?

Not at all! It does not even occupy a specific place in space-time. It might best be described as an oscillating electromagnetic field in space/non-space!

Thus we find that the fundamental property from which the material world is constructed is an illusion. All that remains is that which we, at this very moment, are sharing: thought-energy-intelligence; the unique, particular life form that directs and distinguishes one human being from another, but is, in reality, the whole of the human being.

The British physicist, Sir James Jeans, summed it up when he said, "the universe was looking more like a big thought than a big machine. It may even be that what we think is *real* and the physical universe is just an interference pattern (an impertinent blip) in the world of thought."[40]

In light of what has been said, we can and should extend these notions to its proper perspective in our search for the truth. Fear of truth should be left behind. Kabbalistically speaking, man is no different from the universe in structure. Man's physical body, like the universe, is an interference pattern. This is "the desire to receive for the self alone" which is discerned as the life form of the body. In scientific terms, this energy-intelligence is the particle aspect of the electron. The energy-intelligence of the spirit is given the name, "desire to receive for the purpose of sharing." The electron, when stimulated by man's thought consciousness of a desire to share, turns into a wave.

The former energy-intelligence — for the self alone — corresponds to the "evil" aspect of the Tree of Knowledge. The latter energy-intelligence — for the purpose of sharing — equates with the "good" aspect of the Tree of Knowledge.

The universe — and man in it — is an enormous composite of thought. We may be inclined to think that a thought as huge as the universe could only be held in the mind of the Lord. The Grand Unified Thought which I am addressing is termed in Kabbalistic language, Encircling Light, or wave in scientific terms. It is but a larger all-encompassing manifestation of some individual thought which, we, the author and reader, are sharing at this moment.

The Grand Unified Thought otherwise known as Encircling Light exists in our minds, in our bodies, in everything we experience, taste and touch, see and do. Every force observed, whether particle or anti-particle, matter or antimatter is directed by and acts according to the dictates of a particular intelligence of thought.

One single Light binds together everything in Heaven and Earth. We know that both, plus and minus polarities, are required in nature to complete an electrical energy-intelligent circuit. It follows, that there must also be a balancing counter force in the universe which causes separation and fragmentation, whether we are speaking of the Big Bang or of human relationships. The attributes of separation, fragmentation, time, space, motion and limitation refer to the "evil" segment of the Tree of Knowledge. This segment comprises the perception and thought of particle.

Chaos and decay are only illusionary landmarks in the landscape of particle observation. This flow in the universe was a necessary evil, although for the Kabbalist, this phenomenon remains illusionary.

The souls of man felt ashamed at the one-sidedness of their relationship with the Creator. This condition, which results from receiving that which is not earned, is defined in Kabbalistic terms as Bread of Shame. It was the Creator's wish, and sole purpose, to bestow abundance on his creations. His creations could partake of his abundance only to the degree to which their sense of shame would allow them. The Creator, then — due to the Kabbalistic doctrine of "no coercion" in abundance and spirituality — caused the souls of man to undergo a contraction.[41] This caused a *diversity*, a separation between the Creator and the emanated ones or souls, severing or discriminating the latter from the Former and causing the emanated one to acquire its own particular or particle name. To grasp this is to grasp a Kabbalistic absolute; to master it is to find its wisdom.

Before the contraction or Big Bang, no differentiation of any sort existed. Following the contraction, the Grand Unified Thought became concealed, just as the sun being screened by clouds gives one the illusion that the sun on this cloudy day does not shine. This new cosmic state is referred to as *wave* consciousness or Encircling Light intelligence.

The Encircling Light or Quantum consciousness pervades the entire universe as an uninterrupted, non-fragmented wave. The universe is occupied in large part by wave or anti-matter consciousness. This state of the universe has been designated in the Bible by the code name *Tree of Life*. Those of us who become connected with the Tree of Life state of consciousness do not experience the illusionary defects within the creative process.

This may be likened to a clear electric bulb connected to an electrical circuit. The moment that the light is switched on the poles and filament seem to disappear. The truth of the matter is that the function of the opposing polarities in the filament is illusionary. The light that supposedly appeared after turning on the switch was there in the first place (the cloud problem). Light is a wave and is everywhere, in the middle of a mountain, in the depths of the sea.

Our illusionary perception (the cloud) of the light appears by our intervention, flipping the switch, after which our physical effort then disappears along with the physical components of the bulb. The physical effort involved is only one example among many which indicates that, due to the original contraction (restriction) which came about because of Bread of Shame, we humans were provided with an illusionary creative process that makes everything appear as if we were the creators of things around us.

Consequently, this blanket cover of illusion which supports decay, uncertainty, chaos and limitation, referred to as a particle state, was a necessary "evil" within the creative process. However, this illusionary state of consciousness can undergo a process of correction, reversing the illusionary to a state of "good."

The Tree of Knowledge comprised the two states of consciousness designated by the Bible as "good" and "evil." What exactly did the Bible mean by "evil" and for that matter "good"? Most interpretations of this highly significant and popular section of the Bible have as many commentaries as there are people in this world.

The framework of "evil" embodies all aspects of the illusionary realm, namely, chaos and disorder. From the Kabbalists' standpoint that which is temporary is considered illusionary. Only that which is eternal is considered real. Evil has a thousand faces and yet it has only one, the thought-energy-intelligence of Desire to Receive for the Self alone. Everything that revolves around that deceptive, ever-changing face of Desire, everything that emanates from it, everyone who allows that negative aspect of Desire to prevail, falls under its influence.

Yet, evil has no life of its own. Like a puppet, it is a lifeless, bloodless entity onto which we paint the faces and for which we pull the strings. *We* animate evil and give it substance through our negative thoughts and actions. Yet, despite its myriad of dubious characteristics, even evil may be seen in a positive light. In fact, it may be said that evil is an earthly necessity. For, it is only through restriction of Desire to Receive for oneself alone that Light is revealed. Perhaps, we owe a small debt of gratitude to evil for permitting us the opportunity of absolving Bread of Shame.

Fortunately, reality cannot possibly be negatively influenced by that which is an illusion. Our Encircling Light is connected with the higher realms, the super-conscious Light of the Endless.[42] To connect with this higher world — which is our inalienable right (some might say our duty) to accomplish — usual, habitual thought processes must be transcended.

How? This, therefore, is the objective of the Biblical narrative of the Trees and the Garden of Eden. The Zohar removes the myth surrounding the Tree of Knowledge. The verse seems to imply that Adam was told not to eat of the Tree of Knowledge.[43] However, questions the Zohar, the preceding verse specifically states, "of every tree of the garden, you may eat freely" including the Tree of Knowledge.

Therefore, concludes the Zohar, in truth, Adam was *permitted* to partake of the Tree of Knowledge. However, he was cautioned that when eating of the Tree of Knowledge which consisted of the illusionary realm of chaos, he must also eat of the Tree of Life.

The Tree of Life realm was filament wave consciousness. With restrictive consciousness one combines the "evil" particle consciousness known as the Tree of Knowledge, producing a transformation of particle consciousness to a transcending wave consciousness.

The scientific conclusion, that when a particle meets up with an anti-particle they would annihilate each other, is contrary to the Zoharic interpretation of the Garden of Eden. According to the Zohar, the particle is transformed into a mutual Encircling Light consciousness.

It is the observation of physicists that when particle and anti-particle collide an enormous display of light results. The Kabbalist sees this explosion as a transcending of the particle from its illusionary realm to the wave realm of Encircling Light. The result is not annihilation and chaos, but rather a beautiful display of revealing *Light*.

The explosion, from a Kabbalistic perspective, is the demise and removal of another packet of the illusionary cloud. With each transformation of a particle more light has entered the realm of our universe, hence the result of this activity is light.

Wave consciousness is light. Particle consciousness is illusion. When a physicist observes an electron as a particle, his own personal consciousness of "desire to receive for the self" has stimulated the electron to act as a particle. When the electron behaves as a wave, the observing scientist, at that moment, has thought consciousness of the Tree of Life. His thought wave consciousness is the stimulant that affects the wave behavior of the electron. Thus, the universe, from a Kabbalistic viewpoint, was created in a divine state of pure order and structure, and so it remains. To assert the idea of "randomness" and uncertainty principles as truth, is, to demonstrate an egotistical attitude toward inexplicable phenomena.

According to the ancient Kabbalistic wisdom, there are two parallel universes, one highly ordered, the other random and chaotic. The former is real, the latter illusionary. Yet, both resulted from a single, clearly comprehensible cause.

To achieve a balanced and harmonious integration of these two elements requires a fusion of the Tree of Knowledge with the Tree of Life. This task belongs to mankind. However, we must be aware of that part of ourselves which was born into chaos, while remembering, at the same time, that the greater, more significant, part of ourselves belongs to the unified whole.

The individual preserves his independence while, at the same time, remaining connected with the single, all-pervasive Force. Contrary to appearances, there is no chaos in the universe.

Thus we speak of parallel universes. One is the linear universe, which is ruled by the negative, particle aspect of desire. The other is the circular universe, the realm of wave consciousness, which is revealed through the Desire to Receive for the Sake of Sharing.

These two aspects of desire, which are analogous to the positive and negative poles of a magnet, imparted to us sufficient freedom to relieve Bread of Shame. At the same time, they shackled us with the inability to see things as they really are.

The Kabbalah reveals the natural laws and principles by which to transcend Bread of Shame and access the ordered universe of wave consciousness, the Circles. Past, present and future would reveal themselves to be unified aspects of the Force. There is no empty space, no false state of vacuum, no expanding universe.

Hubble's Law states that the universe is expanding. Other physicists went on to explain the forces responsible for the dispersion of galaxies throughout space. None of their theories gave any indication as to how large a velocity of recession was to be expected.

The objects observed were believed to be moving away from the observer. The view of the universe as an unchanging system, which had persisted from Newton to Einstein, was replaced by an expanding model. One can never see faults in observation until some new circumstances arise or some ingenious person comes along to show us how blind we have been.

Essentially, there are two kinds of scientific misadventures. One starting off on a false trail altogether, the other making temporary blunders along the true path of reality. These observations by scientists infer that the galaxies of the Universe will continue to hurry outward at velocities that steadily decrease but will never reach zero.

Astronomers of the future, we are told, will find fewer visible objects in the evening sky as the galaxies continue their flight into the darkness and space. Subsequent speculation abounds with collapsing universes, reversals in the arrow of time, older persons growing younger and much more.

I can see Kabbalists musing over the efforts of these

astrophysicists, and wondering when will these scientific researchers conclude they have been chasing moonbeams. According to the Zohar, Creation consists of two parallel universes. The physical reality of our celestial bodies are but illusionary. If such is the case, then what is receding where?

Furthermore, from our discussions and conclusions which are consistent with existing scientific knowledge, the view of our galaxies depends upon the consciousness of the observer. Consequently, the fear of a collapsing universe is unfounded. On the contrary, wave mechanics and the idea of our universe turning into a wave indicates we are heading for a Tree of Life rendezvous.

In conclusion, may I again reiterate the intent of writing this chapter. Scientists are unable to explain the efficacy of quantum mechanics, unable to explain it away. The traditional scientist is faced with the unsettling prospect that there must be two realities. Slowly the scientist is being obliged to accept the fact that the laws of science do not apply to the metaphysical, true reality realm.

More importantly, the scientist is being forced to abandon his cherished concept of an objective reality. The problem has been that, for too long, we the laypeople have been led to believe science possesses all the answers. Today we know that no longer is true.

Kabbalistic wisdom does hold out promise for a bright future. We laypeople have the ability to take matters into our own hands, and once again steer our boat through stormy waters and arrive at a destination filled with promise and hope for a bright future.

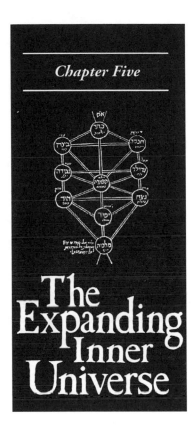

Chapter Five

The Expanding Inner Universe

THE READER MUST BECOME ACQUAINTED WITH HIS invisible surroundings if he is to achieve control over his destiny. To master one's ship is unalterably linked and dependent upon our *knowledge* of the vast expanse of the environment, terrestrial and galactic. Knowledge is the connection[44] and without a complete and *truthful* understanding of our quantum universe, there is no chance that we may change future chaos and disorder in our lives.

The need to make a concentrated effort to become knowledgeable in certain areas of our physical, illusionary world has already been dictated by the Kabbalistic doctrine of Bread of Shame. I know all to well that the average layman has fallen into a complacent attitude of "show me", "present it on a silver platter" and thus avoids the necessity of *earning* this important knowledge.

In this respect we can rightfully place the blame and problem of our dilemma at the doorstep of TV, the *boob tube trap*. Aside from raping our brain faculties and dulling the mind, it has robbed us of much valuable time that could and should be spent more wisely. I have made every effort to present scientific data in a way that would allow the least initiated follower of science to come to grips with.

To think that Kabbalistic teachings will come as a gift to those who make *n o* attempt or effort to understand the complexities is fanciful. At the same time, I might add, with a little labor and trouble, the wonderful world of Kabbalah becomes available to all those who seek it. And, in our day and age, who can deny the necessity for control over our existence laden with chaos, disorder and uncertainty.

But, you, my reader, may question the validity of my assurance that with a *little effort* you may gain entrance into the profound community of the Kabbalist. No pain, no gain, little pain, little gain is the accepted principle of life's existence. However, since we now live in and experience the Age of Aquarius,[45] the benefits of reaping enormous knowledge with little effort as compared to previous generations is now possible.

Rabbi Shimon bar Yoḥai confirmed that the Messianic Era will bring with it a Light and a richness representing the infusion of the Force through all the worlds. The dawn of a new age will appear and with its advent the Force will begin to liberate Rabbis and scientists from their lack, bringing them spiritual awakening and well-being.[46]

The objective, declares the Zohar, is inextricably connected with *Ḥokhmah* (wisdom) and completely dependent upon the dissemination of true knowledge, the sublime wisdom of the Kabbalah.[47] The Zohar asserts that those individuals searching for a connection with the Force, will be rewarded in the Age of Aquarius with a recognition of the internal relationship between man and the cosmos. With the knowledge of Kabbalah becoming increasingly widespread, a higher consciousness and *expanded* awareness will become the domain of the people.

In the Aquarian Age, we will all be infused with the insight to guide us through illusion to the ultimate, all-embracing reality, the Force. Knowledge of the Force will be the dominion of all.

> Open to me an opening no wider than the eye of
> a needle, and I will open to thee the supernal
> gates.[48]

According to the Zohar, the Aquarian Age will usher in an unprecedented level of knowledge for all people. The simplicity of the universe shall take everyone by surprise. Accustomed to present complex perspectives concerning the origins and building blocks of our universe, the Zohar assures us that these veils of confusion will be lifted. Before our very eyes, the universe will unfold the vast unknown and peel away the clouds of obscurity.

We shall not have any need to delve into the foundations of mathematics or the very nature of physical reality. The Age of Aquarius will reward those individuals *searching* for a connection with the Force with a recognition of the internal relationship between man and the cosmos.

Rabbi Ashlag, the twentieth-century Kabbalist, philosopher, translator of the entire Zohar, contended that breaking through the cloud barrier of uncertainty to expanded consciousness requires only one prerequisite. That prerequisite is desire.

Tradition has stated that when the Ari, Isaac Luria, studied the Zohar, the flame of his desire burned with such intensity that perspiration would quite literally pour off him.[49] Through his studies the Ari absorbed, converted and transformed the *Klippot* (veils), the curtains that prevent the beautiful, simple universe from appearing before us.

The majestic cosmos that lies behind the veiled curtain may be compared to the sun on a cloudy or rainy day. Ask a little child whatever became of the sun and the response would assuredly be, today the sun *does not* shine. Before high flying machines or planes, most of us might have thought the same. However, today, flying through and above these clouds, we have come to the realization that the sun does indeed shine every day, rain or shine. The clouds provide a temporary illusion. So too, with the Tree of Knowledge universe placed within the cosmos for the express purpose of blocking out the beautiful realm of the Tree of Life certainty; we thus have the opportunity to remove the cosmic flaw of Bread of Shame.

Once removed, everything we thought we did not know about our universe becomes beautifully revealed to all who merely seek the knowledge. No degrees or honorariums are necessary for acquiring this simplified view of the universe. That the Ari's efforts were rewarded is evidenced by the fact that Lurianic Kabbalah has survived intact for over four hundred years.

Let us first examine the physical expanding universe as it has been presented by astrophysicists. Following our investigation of their findings and conclusions, we shall then proceed to penetrate the world of our own expanding internal universe-consciousness.

Scientific conclusions have emerged as anything but a neat, systematic progression from theory to observation and then on to testimony and solution. Rather they appear as a confused and complicated process in which theories and assumptions may lead to blind alleys. In most cases observational evidence may challenge theoretical biases, and new discoveries of unimagined phenomena may require new theoretical approaches.

Since science is a human enterprise, it becomes subject to individual egos, prejudices and human mistakes. Despite these shortcomings science demonstrates an unprecedented and over-reactive arrogance towards the wealth of data and variety of explanations provided by the Kabbalah and other esoteric teachings. Precise information needed to understand the principles underlying the very nature of the physical universe have remained largely ignored by ivory-tower insulated scientists.

However, before the presentation of our simplified view of an expanding universe, let us first take a look at what these scientists have to say about the matter of an expanding universe. All scientists are in agreement about one thing. This century has seen an unprecedented expansion in our knowledge about the universe. It easily overshadows the gains made in all the previous centuries combined.

Unfortunately, their mutuality stops there. Their conclusions, and there are many, have been proven to be incorrect. Their theories and observations may conform to the reality of existence, but the paradigm models they set based on their theories are at best illusionary and at least, misleading.

The notion of an expanding universe began a relatively

short time ago, back in the 1930's. One might say that Einstein gave birth to twentieth century physics which grew out of his revolutionary theory of relativity. But the irony was that Einstein, who had unlocked the route to the later expanded quantum theory, rejected outright this new theory. His unique personality could not intellectually accept the premise that reality was governed by chance and randomness. Einstein certainly did not fit the glove of scientific inquiry as we laymen might have suspected. After all, when does one's personal attitude or intellectual ego bear any influence on pure, objective inquiry.

At an early age, he reached the conclusion that much in the stories of the Bible could not be true. The consequence was a fanatic desire to free himself from the shackles of established religion. He made an attempt early on to remove what he considered were the chains of hopes, wishes and feelings.

He erroneously believed that the world "out there" existed independently of us human beings. He could not accept the comfortable and alluring road to the religious paradise. No different from the Kabbalist who cannot come to grips with the Bible as simply a Book which provides comfort and solace in its religiosity, he rejected outright Biblical interpretations for the sake of religion.

Einstein converted from a personal religion to a religion of science. He believed that laws concerning our universe should be known and understood. He therefore replaced religion with science where he felt he could now apply himself independently of his thoughts and feelings. Einstein, like others in his field accepted those laws of material reality only to the extent confirmed by experience.

Einstein held steadfastly to his cherished view of determinism. There was no room for chance or randomness and he could never come to accept the notion of the intervention of human consciousness or the possibility of purpose in the nature and structure of the universe.

When quantum theory destroyed the view of a deterministic world, Einstein resisted the quantum notion that an observer was directly involved with creative reality. Because he wanted a closed, static universe, Einstein eventually made an attempt even to alter his own relativity equations. Later on in life he called this mutilation the biggest blunder of his life.

Edwin Hubble is considered one of the most important astronomers in history. He discovered the discipline of extragalactic astronomy through the use of the 100-inch Mount Wilson telescope. He assembled the observational evidence which clearly indicated that the Universe is not static. Contrary to Einstein's *feelings* that the universe is static — no movement and motionless — Hubble found the dynamics of the universe and that it was expanding in all directions.

Hubble's discovery that all galaxies are receding or moving away from each other is regarded as the outstanding discovery in astronomy of this century. Our sample of the universe is the region of space that we can explore with existing telescopes. Of course, astronomers will never be certain of what lies beyond the limits of their telescopes. Telescopes, in their opinion, justify attempts to infer the nature of the universe from the observed characteristics of the sample available for inspection. This attempt is called the observational approach to cosmology.

The idea of an expanding or receding universe is contradictory to the Kabbalistic view of our universe. And more important, past findings by the elite in astronomy have had no significant impact on universal behavior. The views of the Kabbalists are for only one express purpose, and that is for mankind to achieve control over one's destiny.

Taken all together from the dawn of astronomic investigation and space exploration, the world is in no better shape for all its new discoveries. Certainly, the rocks brought back from the moon have not improved in any way the lifestyle of earth's inhabitants.

Furthermore, I have made an attempt in this chapter to bring home a clear picture for the layman as to how uncertain and inconclusive the fields of physics and astronomy really are. The science sections of all major newspapers are bombarded daily with suggestions of new findings concerning our universe from the elite in their respective fields.

But upon careful examination, the article *always* concludes with the statement, "of course we cannot be certain". My intention, in spending so much of my readers' time and my ink in this connection, is to prepare the reader for a completely new perspective of our cosmos. And more importantly, how these time-proven perspectives of Kabbalah can enhance our well-being; something the uncertain conclusions of astrophysicists have painfully and dismally failed to provide.

Scientists have been guilty of the same kind of neglect as religionists, which is, their failure to ask questions, and more specifically, to know the "why of things" rather than the nature of things. Try asking a religious person programmed since childhood as to the "why" of his many doctrines and his response assuredly will be "so it is". The scientist is equally to blame when confronted with the question as to "why" was there a Big Bang in the first place? His response to this and all other similar questions is that the knowing of why is not the task of the scientist.

In any event, it is not our purpose here to present a treatise on the new physics versus the old, but merely to show the dissension among the ranks of science as it relates to different perspectives of reality. Quantum mechanics veers away from the position that the universe is governed by laws that are susceptible to rational understanding. It places it in a framework of the study of consciousness — and for this the Kabbalist is grateful.

It sees man as a participant, rather than merely an observer of reality — another concept hailed by Kabbalah. For this too, has been a major tenet of Kabbalistic thinking for the past two millennia.

And as for the idea that the observational method can present conclusive determinations regarding our universe, quantum mechanics has completely challenged this scientific method. At the very least, quantum mechanics threatens to evaporate a mirage that has for centuries been generally accepted as reality. That mirage is the *Tree of Knowledge* reality, the cloud that conceals the true reality.

Assuming the universe is expanding, but why should the galaxies be fleeing us? Could there be something special going on, or have we performed some offensive act and they are fleeing for their lives? Then again, the process perceived by an observer may not necessarily be a correct deduction. There is a nagging suspicion among some astronomers that all may not be right with the notion that the universe is expanding.

Today we cannot explore with our telescopes all of the universe, nor do we understand why the universe is receding. All interpretations, and there are many, along with the definitive solution will doubtless await the construction possibly of still larger telescopes.

I think that the fanciful trappings that are found in all scientific undertakings have arisen because of our present level of limited vision. There is no shortage of scientists who will shout this problem down. But then again, we are only human, and our egos do exert a great deal of influence on our decisions.

Nevertheless, as I have mentioned previously, in my opinion, their protestations are more dogmatic than scientific. Their arguments, which hold great sway over the layman, stem in large measure from ideas that were pre-set to begin with from childhood on. Religionists, like scientists, refuse to allow their thinking to develop. What is even worse is their outright rejection of change or the acceptance of new ideas which simplify matters.

Doubts and uncertainty play a greater role in scientific inquiry. Once a new idea comes along, the simpler the idea, the greater the objection to its acceptance. This may sound like a paradox, but unfortunately it is true.

The pre-set state of mind consciousness originates from the Tree of Knowledge realm. Why, may we ask, does this illusionary realm exert a superior influence over our decisions?

The Zohar explains the dynamics behind our vulnerability towards deception, towards finding excuses rather than explanations to life's complexities. Those who stand up for change in what they believe in are among the few, far and in-between.

> The moment a child is born into the world, the negative energy-intelligent inducer immediately attaches himself to it. He remains constantly

under the influence of this force, as it is written, "sin coucheth at the door",[50] the term "sin" refers to the *Yetzer haRa*, the negative entity and "door" to the opening of the womb.

He is so called because he makes man every day to sin before the Force, never leaving him from the day of his birth till the end of his life. The positive energy intelligent inducer comes to man only on the day when man is ready for circuity and energy, to wit, when he reaches the age of thirteen years by a male, and at age twelve by a female.[51]

Note that the animals from the day they are born are able to take care of themselves, and avoid fire and similar dangers, whereas man, on the other hand, seems to feel at first a natural propensity to throw himself into the fire. The reason being that the negative inducer dwells within him and lures him into evil ways.

As it is written, "Better is a poor and wise child than an old and foolish king, who knoweth not how to receive admonition anymore."[52] The "child" here signifies the good inducer, who is so called because he is, as it were, a youngster by the side of man, whom he does not join till he is at the age of thirteen years. He is better, then, than "an old foolish king". To wit the evil inducer, who is called king and ruler over the sons of men, and who is assuredly old, since, as already said, as soon as a man is born and sees the light of day he attaches himself to him; and he is foolish, not knowing how to receive admonition.[53]

What emerges from the Zohar is an in-depth revelation concerning human frailties, what they are, where they come from. Connection with the negative energy-intelligence inducer is the primary reason why people are negative, closed to suggestions, and behave with tunnel vision. Thus, we find our society oriented by that inducer, and seemingly bent upon a self-destruct course. This is the essential purpose for the existence of this negative inducer.

Since the positive energy-intelligence inducer arrives on the human scene at a later date, this permits the negative inducer to settle in and entrench itself within the psyche of the individual Much effort is then required by each of us to begin the task of shaking loose from its clutches and becoming thinking people, a chore most people would rather avoid.

The tidal wave of opposition to new ideas is thus understandable, inasmuch, as all of humankind undergoes this attachment at their birth. The pre-set mind we spoke of previously is the direct result of our negative inducer. An open mind to others and their suggestions originates from the positive side of our inducer. The basis and composite of our negative inducer originates with the intelligence of the "desire to receive for the self alone", the idea of the Tree of Knowledge reality. Limitation, uncertainty is its trademark. New ideas may cause new or additional responsibilities and sharing of these new notions.

Fresh or changing ideas may upset the *apple-cart*, or may result in shifts in our complacent lifestyles. There aren't many out there who are prepared to assume accountability for others, when this may require at times severe hardships and sacrifices.

Society may frown upon those whose desire to receive is for the sake of sharing. Sometimes we refer to them as trouble-makers, yet these individuals remain steadfast in their convictions and are even prepared to surrender their ivory-tower positions.

I have devoted a considerable amount of time and space to show in an objective manner modern scientific viewpoints and the untenability of their viewpoints. Science seems to have driven us to accept that we are all merely parts of a universe governed in full detail by very precise and mathematical laws. They also claim that our brain, which seems to *control* all our actions and what-ever emerges as later physical expressions, is ruled by the same laws. To a certain, *limited* extent, all this is correct.[54]

However, the picture they have conjured up is that all this precise physical activity is nothing more than the acting out of some vast computation. Therefore, our mind and brain are to be understood solely in terms of such computations. Yet, they them-selves, find it hard and have the uncomfortable feeling that there must be something missing from such a picture. There is an apparent dilemma here, one that seems to have no way out.

There is much more to this beautiful scenario than just a group of computers, machine or man, whose purpose is merely to crunch out confusing data. There is mystery and beauty, and most if not all of it resides with concepts that lie within the Kabbalistic perspective of our universe.

That perspective is the wave/particle idea or in Kabbalistic language the Tree of Life/Knowledge realities. Consciousness, which lies at the very heart of these realities is the important phenomenon that we simply should not disregard; unlike Steven Weinberg, astrophysicist, who with disdain believes, that our universe is pointless. Furthermore, he believes the quantum field theory is going to go on being very stubborn in refusing to allow us a description of our world.

According to the Kabbalah, there is, besides this tumultuous "physical reality", another timeless, spaceless reality. This reality operates according to an infinite set of criteria, beyond the machinations of the physical world. This is the Reality to which the Kabbalist aspires.

A number of Kabbalistic concepts are at odds with current accepted scientific theories, and the speed of light happens to be one of them. So far as the Kabbalist is concerned, there is no such thing as the *speed* of light. The essence of Light is everywhere, timeless, all pervading and motionless. This is the *wave* concept that symbolizes the code of reality of the Tree of Life consciousness.

This naturally raises a question that almost asks by itself. If light does not move, then what is it that, for so long, scientists have been measuring? Despite experiments to the contrary, scientists still feel compelled to cling to the notion that light travels, and travels at a speed of 186,000 miles per second. Thus they embrace an illusionary reality if indeed Light is motionless and what they are in fact measuring is the movement on the part of the vessels, the *Sfirot*, which contain and make manifest the already existing light.

A bulb in a "dark" room when lit merely reveals the light that was already present before the switch was turned on. Light is everywhere. And where could something that is everywhere possibly go that it would not already be? And so, while it may be a convenience to think in terms of the Light moving through the various levels of emanation, in truth, Light does not move.

Why should it? Light *lacks* nothing. It needs nothing. It wants nothing. It has no need, consciousness or desire to do anything but share its endless beneficence.

This is what the Ari meant, when he stated, that there is no disappearance of Spiritual Substance. What is spiritual? Spiritual substance is the intrinsic nature of Light which includes everything that is, was or will be — with one exception: the illusion of lack which embodies decay, misfortune, chaos and uncertainty.

Lack and Desire to Receive are synonymous, inseparable, yet both are illusions. Only from our finite perspective do they seem all too real. This corresponds to the Tree of Knowledge reality. The Light or Tree of Life reality has but one aspiration, which is, to give of its infinite abundance.

It is only we, the vessels, who are motivated by the illusion and saddled with its constant companion, Desire to Receive. In *truth*, from the perspective of infinity, we lack nothing. It is only from the finite perspective that we seem to lack the fulfillment which comes from being separated and disconnected from the Tree of Life reality, the Infinite Light.

Everything in this universe, physical and metaphysical was preceded by the Light. All substance is spiritual. Even matter, at its essence level, is spiritual substance. Matter is only a temporary alignment of an atomic structure. The subatomic basis of matter is not of a material nature and is therefore not influenced by physical laws.

Only an infinitesimal fraction of matter falls under the jurisdiction of gravity and the laws described by the physical sciences. This small quantity of matter, from the finite perspective, is deemed non-spiritual. Only that, which is encompassed by a consciousness of Desire to Receive, must suffer through the constant illusion of lack, chaos, disorder and uncertainty and is subject to change, transformation and seeming evaporation. The Light, the Tree of Life reality, is constant and never changing. Spiritual substance never disappears.

Only by transcending rational consciousness can the higher realms of Tree of Life existence be perceived. The physical, Tree of Knowledge, is to the metaphysical Tree of Life as one side of a coin is to the other, apart, yet, at the same time, together. From the finite, illusionary world do words such as time, space, upper, lower, physical and metaphysical have purpose and function.

From the perspective of the Infinite, there are no distinctions, no differentiation, no time, no space, no restriction of any kind. All that exists from the Infinite point of view is cause and effect, the cause being the Light, the effect the desire for which is to receive.

Now for an objective picture of the physical world: We must come to the realization that what we see and observe will depend completely on our conscious state of mind. We must also come to terms with this picture of consciousness. In our diagram of the goblet (page 55) we noticed a constant switch between the goblet and the two figures facing each other.

For many of us, the exchange from one to the other is automatic, almost beyond our control. Noteworthy is the enigma as to why the eyes do not see any movement as the goblet replaces the figures and vice versa. This clearly indicates that the change or switching takes place solely within our consciousness. How else can we explain this transference of one observable entity, the figure (particle), to the background goblet (wave).

In the previous chapter we explained our passing from one survey to the next as a consciousness switch. Man consists of two separate and distinct states of consciousness. There are two levels of man — the internal *soul* consciousness or reality level, and the external body consciousness referred to as the physical, illusionary level.

Prior to the sin of Adam, the entire universe existed and remained connected to the Tree of Life reality, unfettered by claims of space and time, unshadowed by entropy and death. Body consciousness was completely dominated by soul consciousness. Once Adam sinned, he fell from the intrinsic connection with the Tree of Life and was now subject to the Tree of Knowledge reality, where body consciousness with its illusionary influence stood side by side with soul consciousness.

Thus, man's external/internal conflict began. The soul is responsible for a person's creativity, free will, sharing and connection with the wave consciousness of the Tree of Life reality. The illusion of darkness brought on by body consciousness is the cause of problems, difficulties, uncertainty and limitation tapping and accessing into the particle consciousness of the Tree of Knowledge reality.

Soul, or internal consciousness exists as a continuous, eternal circuitry of energy because of its wave consciousness connection to the Tree of Life reality. Body consciousness represents and symbolizes a constant illusion of an interrupted, fragmented flow of energy-intelligence because of its *particle* consciousness connection to the Tree of Knowledge.

Body consciousness, Desire to Receive for the Self Alone,

illusion, and particle or particle consciousness, are all synonymous with each other. The particle represents a precise, defined, and thus limited entity. Extending the particle qualities, it portrays a fragmented, separated existence. At this level of reality, human beings feel separated from each other, body apart from another body. Thus, today appears separated from yesterday and tomorrow. It (particle consciousness) symbolizes the here and now only.

Soul consciousness, the Desire to Share, and wave consciousness are all renderings of the true reality. The motion of wave consciousness describes an endless pervading force almost without beginning or end, where yesterday meets up with tomorrow. Hence, wave consciousness symbolizes continuity, togetherness, a kind of uninterrupted connection with the Lightforce. Thus waves appear as white or translucent sheets spread across an area similar to the blanket rays of the sun.

Thought consciousness is an integral part of all animate and inanimate creation. It directs the activity of the particle. A particle may be expressed as a rock, table, fruit, animal, man and even celestial bodies like the sun and moon. A particle is the Desire to Receive. We therefore distinguish and differentiate between one physical entity and another.

In celestial bodies, the observable, albeit illusionary, physical plane of existence symbolizes the *particle* consciousness of limitation. Their internal, wave quantum, consciousness exists in a single all-inclusive multidimensional plane where past, present and future are unified as a quantum whole.

The existence of the two realities — wave and particle or soul and body consciousness — has already been explained by the Zohar.[55] "As the body of man is divided and subdivided into sections and all are poised upon levels of different magnetic fields and intelligence, by which each react and interact with the other, although remaining independent, so is the entire world based upon parallel and different levels by which each segment, each section of the universe is related and interrelated with each other and upon man rests the entire movement and strings of the universe."

Our only choice is to follow the road maps provided by the Zohar, to achieve at-one-ment (remove the hyphens and receive yet another word of power) with the wave consciousness of the Lightforce.

Two incredible statements emerge from the Zohar now dealt with. Man is the determining director of movement in the universe and man is structured as a carbon copy of everything in that universe. Science probes for answers that religion takes on faith. Kabbalah is the bridge between them.

Without knowing that he was virtually paraphrasing the Zohar, the eminent physicist, Albert Einstein once eloquently defined the role of man in the cosmic scheme.

"A human being is a part of the whole, called by us 'universe', a part limited in time and space. He experiences himself, his thoughts and feelings as something separated from the rest — a kind of optical delusion of his consciousness. This delusion is a kind of prison for us, restricting us to our personal desires and to affection for a few persons nearest to us. Our task must be to free ourselves from this prison by widening our circle of compassion to embrace all living creatures and the whole of nature in its beauty."

Einstein, himself, did not comprehend the depth of what he was defining. Had he indeed understood, he might have begun to fathom and understand the true significance of what has been termed an "expanding universe". I find this to be true of all twentieth century physicists. They fail to pull together all of the available data and knowledge to draw the proper and meaningful conclusions about our universe.

Let us therefore investigate their ideas concerning the "expanding universe" and how they have been unsuccessful in determining what is really going on around us.

The distant galaxies in the universe are all receding from us. What this actually means is, that the empty space in the universe, or the wave, is seemingly expanding, is becoming larger. The space between particles or celestial bodies seems to expand.

The information provided by the Zohar, taken all together presents an entirely different perspective of what is superficially observed as an expanding universe. Let us review briefly just exactly what it is, that convinced astrophysicists that the galaxies are receding from each other.

The notion, that the universe is expanding, hinges on the visual equivalent of a familiar characteristic of sound. Sound waves from a receding source are of a lower pitch than those from one that is approaching. The faster a galaxy is moving away from us, the lower is the intensity of its light.

What this shows is that a particle, placed at any point in space, recedes from the observer, with its rate of recession increasing with its distance from the observer. It would seem that the expansion of the universe is just another among many theories that the world will come to an end sooner than we thought. The present orthodox concept of our universe as a kind of inert universe is still a major headache for its supporters.

Just how far the universe has been running is anyone's guess. Unfortunately, the answers concerning our universe appear to be turning out as dusty ones. The results of their investigations and worthwhile significance seem to be elusive. Astrophysicists who believe that the ultimate cosmological problem has been more or less solved may well be in for more surprises.

Physicists now feel the need for some new assumptions on which to build up a theory of cosmology. This need is and will be satisfied by the Kabbalistic perspective which Kabbalists call the unified principle of wave consciousness and the fragmented principle of particle consciousness.

> Said Rabbi Judah: When it says that the "writing was graven upon the tablets",[56] it means that the tablets were pierced, so that the writing could be seen from either side; the writing formed an engraving within an engraving!

> According to Rabbi Abba, it was possible from one side to see the other side, and read the writing. Said Rabbi Elazar: They were written miraculously in order that every man might discern that it was the *"Lightforce's writing"*, since man would be unable to find any other explanation of this double appearance.

> Besides, continued Rabbi Elazar, if the tablets were pierced, as has been suggested by Rabbi Judah, why doesn't the verse say that the writing was graven *"in"* the tablets instead of *"upon"* the tablets, indicating the possibility of viewing the tablets from either side and observing either side from one side.

The fact of the matter is that five commandments were written on the right and five on the left. Those of the left were *included* in those of the right. And from within the right, one could see those of the left, so that all was on the right and all were fused one with the other.

He who stood at one side could see what was on the other side and read it, for we have been taught that the left was turned into the right. Thus it was, indeed, "the writing of the Lord".

What happened was this: he who stood on one side read, "I am the Lord" and out of these letters he could see the words, "Thou shalt not murder". Then he read, "Thou shalt not have other gods", and at the same time could see the words, "Thou shalt not commit adultery"! Then he went on reading, "Thou shalt not take the name of the Lord in vain", and saw from the other side the words, "Thou shalt not steal", and so on, and *conversely*, if he looked at the other side.

The question then arises, how is it possible that the words of the scroll were observable from any direction? Furthermore how do we come to understand the difficult problem of the uniformity and homogeneity of the commandments of the right with the commandments of the left?

One would expect that when looking from behind the scroll the letters would appear in reverse order. Did you ever notice the letters of an ambulance written on the front of the car? They are written in mirror vision. Only when we view the words through a mirror do the words appear in their proper order. And yet, the Zohar maintains that when scanning the scroll, one could see the letters from any position.

In addition, the Zohar's startling revelation that the commandments on the left are somewhat present together with the commandments on the right side, superimposed, a genuine hybrid of the two. Moreover, this hybrid reality is not simply the sum total of the two concepts, but rather an alliance between these two opposite states of consciousness.

Look at the waves of the ocean. What we see are individual waves which seem to move right through each other. The heights of the waves simply add up to give the total height. The principle of adding wave amplitudes to get the total is called the superposition principle. It is important to realize that energy packets or fields of energy do not behave like a water wave. The interpretation, by the noted physicist Max Born, of quantum waves meant the end of determinism and classical objectivity. Physicists began to recognize the radical nature and weirdness of quantum.

Before proceeding to explain the revolutionary ideas of the Zohar there is yet another notion that must first be explored. I am referring to the concept of light which to this day has been a subject treated by all physicists who, to their chagrin, still find it elusive.

Einstein found that if he were to obtain the desired results in his formulation of the Relativity Theory, it was necessary to assume that the velocity of light, as measured by any observer, was always constant. Even before Einstein, physicists knew the speed of light was very fast, about 186,000 miles per second. But Einstein thought there was something *special* about the speed of light. The speed of light was an absolute constant.

Just what did this mean? In simple words, the speed of light was the same whether one was moving towards a source of light or away from it. Also, the same result would be obtained whether the light source was in motion or still with respect to an observer.

Let's assume one person with a flashlight is on a train traveling at a speed of 100 miles per hour and another person is holding a flashlight on the train platform. At the same moment the train passed the person on the platform, both turned on their flashlights directed toward a specific target. The velocity of light as measured by the observer was always constant.

The two velocities must be added. Yet, according to Einstein, light did not behave in this manner. If one made an attempt to add to the velocity of light by causing it to be discharged from a moving source, it would still move at a speed of 186,000 miles per second. Einstein suggested that light, indeed, had its peculiarities.

To appreciate how unusual this really is, imagine that a gun fires a bullet at high speed. The speed of a bullet, unlike the speed of light, is not an absolute constant. If we take off after the bullet in a rocket ship, we should be able to catch up with it.

There is no *absolute* meaning to the speed of a bullet because it is always relative to the speed of the rocket ship. When we catch up to the bullet it appears to us as if it has stopped moving. Not so with light. Its speed is absolute, always the same, completely independent of our own velocity. This is the peculiar property of light that makes its speed different from the speed of anything else.

Another example of *no* absolute meaning to speed is,

when we are in an automobile, stopped at a traffic light. Keeping our foot on the brake pedal, we suddenly notice the car is rolling back, and we continue to press harder. Only after we realize, that the car alongside us had begun to move forward, do we realize that the car we are in was not rolling backwards at all.

Due to the absolute constancy of the speed of light, if alongside us is a beam of light instead of an automobile, we would not experience a feeling of rolling back. Once Einstein established this incredible theory, then interpretations involving the speed of light became a field day for science fiction authors.

Consequently, theories formulated on the basis of observations can and do turn out badly because it is all too easy to fit theories to *already-known facts*. The situation, however, is different when it comes to a theory *predicting* the results. The history of science is riddled with initially convincing theories which have been upset by their own attempts at validation.

Therefore, the first and foremost conclusion of Kabbalistic teachings is that light is indeed different from any other physically expressed entity. Agreeing with the idea of light being constant as postulated by Einstein and all subsequent scientists, the Zohar takes this idea one step further and declares that "there is no movement whatsoever in light."

As weird as this declaration may sound to physicists, they should remember that the whole of quantum is referred to as quantum weirdness. I should hope that this Zoharic idea, that Light is infinite and thus not limited or subject to the impressions of the five senses including observation, will finally become accepted as the true version of our universe.

How did we know that Newtonian classical physics was

not actually a true perspective of our world? The main reason was empirical. Quantum physics was the last resort sought by theorists. Scientists, including Einstein in the latter part of his life, reluctantly agreed to what emerged as an unsatisfying view of our world.

The root cause of the new observation was that the scientists discovered that two kinds of physical objects exist and that they must coexist: fields or waves requiring an infinite number of parameters and particles of small, finite parameters. Another question was, how is it that light can consist of particles and of field oscillations at the same time? These two ideas seem irrevocably opposed.

As if this were not confusing enough, in 1923 the French physicist Prince Louis de Broglie took the particle/wave dilemma one step further by proposing that the particle of matter should sometimes behave like a wave. According to de Broglie the dichotomy between particles and fields is not respected by nature. Nature provides the wherewithal to maintain a world in which particles and waves are sometimes the same and sometimes not.

It becomes quite apparent that nature's universe consists of some subtle ingredients. The language of physics, *particles* and *waves,* conveys but partially appropriate pictures. The language of Kabbalah assigns the whole idea of quantum to consciousness.

Particles are defined as either the "desire to receive for the self alone" (evil) or "Desire to receive for the sake of sharing" (good) encoded within the Tree of Knowledge paradigm. Waves or field-oscillations are the infinite, eternal and motionless state of Encircling Vessels and Lights[57] encoded within the Tree of Life paradigm where light and vessels are unified as one complete whole.

The two-slit experiment, with monochromatic light is the archetypical quantum-mechanical experiment which produced quantum weirdness. This experiment, provided the physicist with a glimpse of quantum's extraordinary implications. The results of this experiment have no analogue in the classical world of everyday sense awareness and are the essential foundation for quantum weirdness.

What was so strange about this experiment? It implied an observer-created reality. The quantum weirdness lies in the realization that so long as we are not actually detecting an electron, its behavior is like a wave. The moment we see the electron it behaves as a particle. No ordinary idea of objectivity can accommodate this weirdness. This new aspect of reality reveals what Kabbalists have known all along: the only reality is consciousness.

What has emerged from the latest conclusions of science is that the specific perceptions of our five senses as the fundamental concepts of physics have finally been eliminated from science. Some scientists still insist on "not letting go." They continue to insist on the primacy of the senses and remain horrified at the thought that all that remains of reality is consciousness.

Max Planck, the famous German Nobel Laureate, insisted that it is incorrect to infer that no fundamental laws of the universe exist because of our inability to grasp them.[58] Sir James Jeans, famous British mathematician wrote: "We can experiment with light, and obtain results which are expressible in terms of the familiar concepts, waves and particles. However, the experiments do not provide for us what the true nature of light is. They do not tell us that it consists of waves or of particles. They merely show us light behaving in a way which reminds us sometimes of waves and sometimes of particles. It may be, that the true nature of light is forever beyond our powers of imagining. Thus we cannot reason about light, only about the results of our experiments with light."[59]

How refreshing and welcome is the revealing Kabbalistic view of the nature of light and its implications for the enhancement of daily living. What does the Ari, Rabbi Isaac Luria, have to say on the subject of Light?

According to the Ari, the physical world is just a blip on the endless screen of reality, a temporary static disruption, a minor disturbance of the Endless Light, a pattern of interference which has existed only for the flash of an instant.

> Before the emanation and creation of the worlds, the Endless Light was all pervading, encompassing all and fulfilling any empty space. The Light is infinite without beginning or end and is referred to as the Light of the Endless. There was no empty space or vacuum. Light is everywhere and there was nothing to add to the Light.[60]

Light is everywhere. Where could something that is everywhere go to, that it isn't there already. Light lacks nothing, it wants for nothing, it needs nothing. Light has no need or desire or consciousness to do anything but share and impart its endless beneficence. Light is a pure unadulterated consciousness with a thought energy-intelligence desire of only sharing, extending, giving whenever an illusionary empty space seems to exist.

This is what the Ari means when he states that there is no disappearance of Spiritual Substance. Spiritual Substance is of the Light, eternal, never-changing, and manifesting only good. The illusion which we experience is ever-changing and can have characteristics of lack, imperfection, faultiness, defectiveness, insufficiency and limitation.

Lack and Desire to Receive are synonymous, inseparable. Like body and soul, energy consciousness and matter, one cannot exist without the other. Yet both are illusions. Only from our finite perspective do they seem all too real. The Light has but one aspiration which is to give of its infinite abundance just as the flame of a candle which can light other unlit candles and not fear any loss in the flame.

It is only we, the vessels, like the wax of the candle, who experience the illusion of lack and seem to undergo the process of disappearance and are saddled with its constant companion, Desire to Receive. In truth, it is only from the finite perspective that we seem to lack fulfillment. This comes about because of our *separation* from the Infinite Light.

The essence of all substance is Light and is therefore spiritual. Matter at its internal level of existence, is the consciousness of the Light to share. Matter on the gross level is a temporary alignment of an atomic structure.

The primal subatomic basis of matter is not, nor has it ever been, of a material nature and, therefore, is not subject to or influenced by any physical laws. Even subatomic units are called "quanta", meaning things, but are more accurately described as *tendencies* to become. And who can touch a tendency, taste it, see it?

Only an *infinitesimal* fraction of matter falls under the jurisdiction of gravity, and the laws described by the physical sciences. This small quantity of matter, from the finite perspective, is deemed non-spiritual, particle consciousness, or the Desire to

Receive for the Self Alone. Only that which is encompassed by the Desire to Receive for the Self Alone must suffer through the constant illusion of lack. Lack, or particle consciousness is subject to transformation, change and apparent decay, uncertainty and disappearance. Light or wave consciousness is constant and never changing.

We have become attached to and overwhelmed by particle consciousness which is an illusion. So accustomed are we to thinking in terms of time, space and motion, that it is impossible to grasp a reality in which dimensions do not exist.

Only by transcending rational, particle consciousness can the higher, infinite realm of existence be perceived and accessed into. How does one go about achieving this transcendence from the particle level of consciousness to the Light-wave consciousness?

The only *light* that we see and the only Light of the Endless (wave consciousness) that we can perceive and experience is *reflected* light. Both upper (Endless Light) and lower light (material) require resistance or restriction in order to be revealed.

Resistance appears and exhibits its energy-intelligent consciousness in a dual manner, involuntary and voluntary. Sunlight is revealed through automatic, unintentional, robotic resistance. Involuntary functions are rooted in the finite particle realm of existence. Trees, animals, our bodies, are not required to excercise deliberate, intentional restriction to manifest the light of the sun. A mirror is not obliged to consciously reflect the light that comes towards it. Our bodies are likewise visible without our having to constantly will their physical appearance. Nor do we have to tell our hearts to continue beating or remind our lungs to continue breathing. We are, however, required to impose conscious resistance[61] in order to reveal the Endless Light.

Of all that exists on this earth, only the human species is obliged to exercise deliberate resistance to reveal the Light. The reason that we are required to act intentionally to *resist* the Light, is to furnish us with the opportunity of removing Bread of Shame. The Endless Light permeates all existence, but like sunlight it only becomes visible when reflected.

To reflect the light — to behave with restriction — is to reveal the Light, and to become at-one-ment with wave consciousness. To not reflect means remaining in the spiritual darkness of *particle* consciousness. The paradox is that by rejecting the Light one receives It. By expressing our particle consciousness of "Desire to Receive for the self alone", one is severed from Its endless beneficence of wave consciousness and all that this portrays as stated earlier.

Concerning this enigma, a relevant physical analogy can be drawn between a *black*, absorbent surface, the motivating energy-intelligence of particle consciousness which is the Desire to Receive for the Self Alone, and a white, reflective surface, the energy-intelligence of wave (*white*) consciousness which is the Desire to Receive for the Sake of Sharing.

Remember our diagram of the goblet? The silhouettes were blank representing particle consciousness, whereas the white background portrayed a wave consciousness. The color black captures light, and because of its particle consciousness it allows as little light as possible to escape. Consequently, in warm climate areas rooftops are colored white thereby diffusing the sunlight into a wave, rather than allowing a particle consciousness concentration of the sunlight.

So too does the greedy person, guided and motivated by the particle consciousness of the Desire to Receive for the Self Alone, hold *captive* the Light that enters his life. He consumes as much as is humanly possible, while giving little in return. For this sort of behavior the reward is the attachment to the Evil, limited, chaotic uncertainty-realm of the Tree of Knowledge reality.

The color white, contrarily, resists and reflects light, thus sharing illumination with any and all in its immediate proximity. Therefore it can be said that the person whose motivating energy-intelligence is of wave consciousness, whose Desire to Receive is for sharing, clings to the Good, infinite, orderly certainty-realm

of the Tree of Life reality. He draws to himself the restrictive consciousness energy of the Tree of Life reality, which is our gateway to the Infinite Light of the Endless.

This sort of person *emulates* the white, reflective surface of wave consciousness. He accepts only what is necessary for sustenance. He does not consider his possessions or wealth as *captives*, but rather as being entrusted with a fiduciary responsibility to share all that remains above what he considers to be his necessities.

This individual need never fear that his sharing may

result in a diminishing of his assets. The Infinite Light will always replenish the assets that have been dispensed with. We may say the fiduciary deposits will keep coming. He has accessed into the wave consciousness of the universe.

When mankind begins to transform particle consciousness into wave consciousness, the result is an increase in the revelation of the Light and a decrease in particle consciousness. With each passing activity of resistance and the Desire to Receive for the Sake of Sharing, particle consciousness begins to diminish and wave consciousness begins to increase and expand.

Mankind, in this Age of Aquarius, will reap the benefits of a two thousand year effort by spiritual people throughout the centuries to transform their Desire to Receive for the Self Alone to one of a Desire to Receive for the Sake of Sharing. Again in the Age of Aquarius, mankind will return to this level of consciousness achieved by the people of the Exodus, when they stood at Mount Sinai.

The slaves of the Exodus were dramatically elevated to an energy-intelligence of wave consciousness. They left behind them the energy-intelligence of particle consciousness with its fruit, the limited, chaotic version of our universe wracked with pain and suffering.

The existence and idea of wave consciousness was already noted by the Kabbalists when they considered the following Biblical verse and the commentary in the Zohar.[62]

> AND ALL THE PEOPLE SAW THE SOUNDS, AND THE
> LIGHTENING, AND THE SOUND OF THE SHOFAR.[63]
> Said Rabbi Abba: The verse says they *saw*, when
> surely it should have stated they *heard* the

sounds. We have been taught that the voices were delineated, carved out as it were, upon the three-fold aspects of darkness, cloud and fog, so that the voices could be apprehended as something visible [like a physical yet nonphysical body] and from this sight that they saw, they were irradiated with a supernal light and perceived things beyond the ken of all succeeding generations. And whence did they derive the power to see? According to Rabbi Yose, from the *Light* of those voices, for there was not one of them but emitted light which made perceptible all things hidden and veiled, and even all the generations of men that will appear up until the days of Messiah. Therefore it is stated: "And all the people saw the voices"; they did *actually* see them [future generations of people.]

The word *Koloth* (voices) is preceded by the particle *eth*, which as usual, indicates that we are to understand another object in addition to the one mentioned; in this case another voice from below, the *Shekhinah* [the universal consciousness] emanating from the other voices in which they saw, in sublime wisdom, all the celestial treasures and all the hidden mysteries which were never revealed to succeeding generations, and will not be revealed until the Messiah comes when "they shall see eye to eye".[64]

What seems to emerge from the preceding Zohar is that once the Hebrews achieved an affinity with the Shekhinah, they were tapping the collective consciousness of the universe. At this level they saw "all succeeding generations", they perceived the universal wave consciousness where tomorrow co-exists with the present and the past.

When they "saw the voices", they were in effect connecting with the internal consciousness of sound. Sound symbolizes a particle type of consciousness with limiting degrees. The internal energy-intelligence of sound connects with universal wave consciousness, where the infinite realm of the Tree of Life reigns supreme.

The Zohar refers to particle consciousness by the expressions "darkness", "cloud" or "fog". They shroud, veil and create an illusion that a wave consciousness does not seem to exist. The Light appears to be concealed. The Hebrews, however, in their elevated state of consciousness now grasped and connected with the Light thereby actually seeing the internal consciousness of the sound as it penetrated, moving aside the particles in its path. The clouds were dispersed by the Light wave consciousness similar to the removal of the darkness in a room when the lights are turned on.

We can all remember when we were very young that on a cloudy day we assumed the sun did not shine that day. Today, we know that that is incorrect. Most of us have experienced rising above the clouds in an airplane to find the sun shining in all its glory.

On Mount Sinai, they "saw" the sound remove clouds and darkness. Particles or physical expressions are nothing more then illusionary barriers that prevent our soul consciousness from connecting with the realm of the Infinite Light. When, however, our soul consciousness maintains a level of constant sharing without interference or interruption from our body consciousness, then a wave or light consciousness pervades enabling the fortunate ones to be connected with the benefits of the Endless Light.

Thus, there is no difficulty in comprehending how the Hebrews could read the letters of the Scroll from either the front or back of the Scroll. The letters themselves represent the particle aspect of the Scroll. From this level of comprehension, it is quite obvious that one cannot read the same letters from either side.

However, when perceiving the internal, wave consciousness of the letters, then its consciousness no longer is one of a finite dimension with our usual perceptive limitations of space and motion. They are there and everywhere. The letters are then transformed from place to place when they are subject to the dominion of wave consciousness. The letters themselves now must conform to the rigid principles of endless and infinite dimensions.

Consequently, the particle consciousness must lose its identity within the wave consciousness just as the silhouettes of the two faces become lost and integrated within the white wave of the goblet.

Perhaps the best way to understand the integration of particle matter into a wave and its subsequent disappearance is to imagine the surf coming onto a beach, where there is a large rock protruding. The waves that arrive at that part of the beach are different from the waves arriving at a smooth beach.

The rock (in this case the particle) changes the waves. In these changed waves we see the rock, as we see the silhouettes in our illustration.

What really is happening is the collision course of the wave and rock intercepting each other. So long as both, the rock and the wave, retain their independent consciousness, each affect the movement and appearance of the other.

On the other hand, a tiny pebble has no appreciable effect on the waves. This small particle just about disappears in the onslaught of the waves.

Another example that may clarify for the reader the idea of how a particle may disappear into a wave is to examine the way the scanning-probe microscopes work. The basic operation involves directing light onto a particle and then taking it into a lens system that produces a magnified image of the particle.

There is a limit to how small an object can be, to be seen with an optical microscope. The reason for this is quite understandable. Light is a wave, and the more we try to focus our microscope on something very small, like a single molecule such as DNA or a single atom, we'd have difficulty distinguishing the atom from the light.

The target would have no effect on the light waves as they were passing by. Like the pebble, it would become invisible by the wave-like actions of the light.

Behind this dynamic interplay of light waves or surf waves is the fundamental idea of a conflict between the consciousness of each. The waves, irrespective of their observable surface, involve an intrinsic, internal metaphysical consciousness of the "desire to receive for the sake of sharing." This, in effect, is the elusive anti-matter that scientists speak so much about and know so little about.

Particle matter is governed by an internal consciousness,

the "desire to receive for the self alone". As predicted by the Zohar, in the Age of Aquarius we can expect an unprecedented transformation from the "Self Alone" to one of Sharing. This, in effect, will produce the fusion of particle matter into the light wave expression.

Like the pebble disappearing into a wave, in this Age of Aquarius we are witnessing the gradual reduction of matter. How? If there is one word that could define advanced technology, the concept of reductionism would say it all. The race for small components in hi-tech is in full swing. The smaller the product, the greater the chances of success.

Common sense tells us that a communication cable's capacity should shrink as its diameter becomes smaller. In the case of fiberoptics, common sense is wrong. Hair-thin fiber optics transmit more calls over longer distances than their bulkier predecessors.

Less is more, the sign of Aquarius. This concept takes some getting used to. This metaphysical paradox goes against the grain of contemporary popular culture. The denser the physical matter the greater the illusion.

Let us now return to the subject of an expanding universe. Essentially, the cosmos reflects the activity of man. The idea of a universe out there, independent of human participation has already been ruled out by the Quantum theory. If this be the case, then what appears as an expanding universe, now becomes another signpost along the route of life's road map.

In essence, the notion that the universe is expanding is an illusion. Reality isn't always what we may want it to be, or what our five senses suggest. The universe is indeed a strange, mystical place in which past, present and future coexist.

Consequently, the conclusion of an expanding universe contradicts the time coexistence factor. The space-time paradigm then comes into question. Change, as the idea of expansion suggests, cannot be expressed at the reality level. Change is a consciousness reserved for the illusionary level of reality. Change seems to occur when we are in that state of consciousness which is "Desire to Receive for the Self Alone."

We stated that wave consciousness is the expression of the Desire to Receive for the Sake of Sharing. Thus waves, wavelengths, light waves, including the vast expanse of space, are considered the physical expression of the Lightforce. Therefore, they represent the world of reality on a terrestrial level and do not undergo any change or expansion.

In our Age of Aquarius particle consciousness is becoming greatly reduced by man's current positive activity of sharing with the added accumulation of positive activity from past generations. Celestial bodies are undergoing a particle integration with the vast expanse of space. Therefore, it seems as if the universe is expanding. Relative to the physical, particle celestial bodies are presently experiencing a diminishing of particle consciousness (the desire to receive for the self alone). Consequently, the stars and planets appear to be moving away from each other. In actuality, the celestial bodies are becoming smaller. As a result of reduced particle consciousness, celestial bodies have turned from a rock to a pebble.

Essentially, all forms of a material nature really do not exist so long as we are not conscious of their existence. This revolutionary way of thinking is part of Quantum theory. Chaos, disorder and uncertainty are by-products of particle consciousness.

The moment mankind makes the decision to transform the Desire to Receive *for the Self Alone* to one of *for the Sake of Sharing*, then particle consciousness, like the pebble, becomes integrated and disappears into a wave. Wave consciousness, connected with the Lightforce then taps the awesome power of the Light which, when revealed, removes the darkness and clouds of uncertainty and chaos.

This then is the message of the Zohar for us in an Age of Aquarius: Restrict and share, thereby affecting everyone and everything around us, including our cosmos. Our daily activities are directly responsible for the particle experience of chaos and uncertainty. Act with the Tree of Life consciousness, and we assuredly achieve certainty and order in our lives.

I trust and pray that this chapter will be fully understood so as to permit a new world order of wave consciousness to set into our environment. I have made an attempt to present some revolutionary ideas from the Zohar, without which we are left with no chance for improvement or enhancement in our daily living. The thousands of years behind us clearly demonstrate that our past and present thinking have only brought pain and suffering to all of mankind.

To make any real changes requires a complete transformation of the way we view the reality around us. Furthermore, in this Age of Aquarius, the cosmos, states the Zohar, will assist and support us in achieving a change in human behavior. Mankind will suddenly realize the folly of particle consciousness. The notion of a desire to receive for the self alone will no longer prevail as the method of fulfillment. The paradoxical nature of the desire to receive for the sake of sharing will become unmistakably the only path by which to achieve the fulfillment of our dreams and aspirations.

The year 1990 will go down in history as the beginning of the power of wave consciousness. In that year dramatic revolutions took place without the firing of a shot. There has been no time in history when such occurrences did not result in the suffering of bloodshed and imprisonment.

In the year 1991, the Gulf war was predicted to be the most violent and devastating war in history. Once again in the Middle East, the future would be written in blood. An estimated 17,000 troops would die during the first hour of battle. This time however, the Age of Aquarius demonstrated the phenomenon that light wave quantum mechanics will assist and support the forces of "good" over the practitioners of evil.

What is required, according to the Zohar, are practitioners who are capable of transforming particle consciousness to that of wave consciousness. The knowledge, tools and equipment are readily available. All systems are go. The only prerequisite, is an effort by mankind to transform the internal self of particle consciousness to one of a sharing wave consciousness.

The effort to contain evil forces that spring forth around us is not an acceptable remedy. We have been programmed since childhood to believe that the good Lord always provides for those who believe in Him. Yet, wherever we turn, misery and chaos appear as mankind's trademark.

We are not puppets in the hands of a puppeteer. A complete transformation of our way of thinking is required. In this Age of Aquarius, this objective is within our reach and is attainable. The future rests with mankind's consciousness and its perspective of our universe. That which we believe exists; this is what reality is all about. We are what we think.

A belief in armed force as a method in resolving conflicts, like most bad news, can be a self-fulfilling prophecy. If you believe it's going to happen, it will. If you refuse to let it happen, it won't.

Yet we cannot afford to close our eyes to existing realities. We know, for example, that for the past decade there have been 36 conflicts in the world each year. There have been internal civil wars and wars between nations. There is a great deal of pressure to resolve these conflicts, but to no avail.

But we can offset this negative approach by adhering to the basic principle that, only with the revelation of the Lightforce, will change in consciousness of mankind take place. To the degree and level that the Lightforce reveals itself, will the people come around to the j essential idea of "Love thy neighbor".

If in this Age of Aquarius the intensity reaches a level too powerful to handle, then mankind will find no other alternative but to alter their particle consciousness to one of wave consciousness. Confirmation of its power will not ever be a decisive factor. Miracles have never been an influence for change. For some of our stubborn brethren, a feeling of having their fingers stuck in an electric socket all day may be the only route to achieve an altered level of consciousness. This environmental condition may be avoided, provided mankind chooses to pursue the spiritual path of revealing the Lightforce.

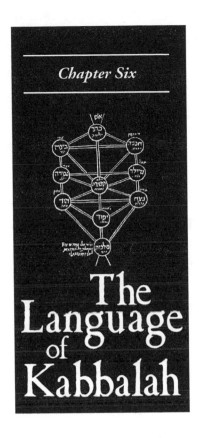

Chapter Six

The Language of Kabbalah

"AND THE WHOLE EARTH WAS OF ONE LANGUAGE AND OF UNITY."[65]
That all of mankind made use of a common language may strike a
strange chord within all of us. Yet this is the recorded statement in
the Biblical narration of the Tower of Babel. Language was formed
some two thousand years prior to the creation of Adam.[66] The
basic building blocks of this language were the Aleph Beth provided by the Biblical text.

The purpose of this particular language was to provide a
means of communication with the subconsciousness of every life
form, be it the human race, the animal kingdom, the celestial or
the extraterrestrial entities. The Aleph Beth and the words structured by it provide an unlimited vocabulary. Its letters and words
transcend the limited realm of our consciousness. They could

clarify and express more precisely the terms of our thoughts and the observable world around us. More importantly, a discussion between two life forms was unmistakably understood between them.

Terms of ordinary language used in the Biblical text that might otherwise provide adequate descriptions have no descriptive value in translation. "And the Lord spoke to Moses" is one example of the difficulty we encounter once we have translated the Hebrew into English. How does one comprehend or come to grips with the language used in the discussion between the Lord and Moses?

Another bizarre discussion, this one between Abram and the Lord, concerns one of a physical nature.

> And the Lord brought him [Abram] outside and said, Look now toward heaven, and count the stars, if thou be able to number them; and He said unto him, So shall thy seed be. And he believed in the Lord; and He counted it to him for righteousness.[67]

The dialogue between the Lord and Abram seems to indicate a normal conversation between two individuals, almost as if both were conversing in Abram's home. What, however, is *outside* or *inside* to the Lord? As the Omnipotent Creator, he is all pervading and omnipresent, the all-inclusive positive energy-intelligence discussed in detail in *Kabbalah for the Layman, Vol. I.*[68]

The shift from that metaphysical reality to the metaphor of the physical plane introduced the anthropomorphic Lord upon which all great religions have since been based, with damaging effects. In this dialogue with Abram, the Creator appears to be cast as one approaching human form. Thus, it becomes incumbent upon us to remember that his presence is all-pervading, despite the language. The Lord is pure energy, devoid of physical form. The concealment of the Lord in an anthropomorphic image is to be understood by the Kabbalistic maxim: that which is to be revealed must first be concealed.

The Kabbalistic decoding of the word "Lord" (*Yud Hei Vav Hei*) indicates an all-pervading, intelligent, conscious-energy force, present in everything in and around us. Thus when the word "Lord" appears in the Bible, it is a personal, intimate concept which provides the possibility of our connecting, and enhances the possibility of creating an affinity, with the Creator.

The language of the Bible, while coded, nevertheless provides us with a useful system by which we can tap its awesome energy. The Zohar furnishes the definitions.

Upon closer examination of the Biblical text, we come upon several names of the Lord. Strange as it may appear, the Bible makes use of various words to address the Lord. An obvious question that must be raised at this time is, why does the Bible refer to the Lord by different names?

Each name, whether it is the tetragrammaton, *Elokim, Ad'nai*, or any one of the other names associated with the Lightforce of the Lord, is merely a word structure indicating another level or intensity of the all-embracing Lightforce.

The planets, stars, milky way or signs of the constellations, are, from a Kabbalistic viewpoint, various expressions of the Lightforce. So too, the various names of the Lord sometimes express the Lightforce as a compassionate force and at other times as one of anger.

The Lightforce itself does not change or undergo any changes, nor does It have any movement. To the Kabbalist the Lightforce is ever present and pervades the entire universe, despite our inability to see It. When a mechanism or instrument, such as the light bulb reveals the Lightforce, we erroneously conclude that the light seen has come into existence only with the throwing of a switch. The Kabbalist views the light as having always been there in the first place. The various systems that reveal the Lightforce are given their appropriate names thus indicating or identifying the way the Lightforce is exposed or manifested.

Everything of a particle nature is nothing more than an expression of the Lightforce itself. A single all-pervasive Force is the motivating and sustaining influence of all existence, physical and metaphysical, illusionary and real.

Only the illusionary aspect of existence behaves in a random manner. The real aspect, the Force, or Endless Light, (*Or En Sof*) is constant, eternal, and entirely predictable. The Lightforce has but one aspiration, and that is, to share its endless beneficence.

Contrary to appearance, there is no chaos in the universe. The language of Kabbalah deals with those particles of nature that form, or consist of, the Tree of Life nature. The Hebrew names given to parts of the body or to regions of the celestial realm reveal the internal nature of the entity, when properly decoded. These names like the heart, the sun or man refer to the manner in which the Lightforce is being expressed. There is no language describing the Lightforce itself other than the Kabbalist term Endless Light.

We do know that the underlying nature of the Lightforce is one of sharing. However, all other expressions require the attachment of a name. We must give the "baby" a name. The language of Kabbalah, in addition to providing a name for all expressions of the Lightforce, also affords a window to the internal energy-intelligence of that particular entity.

It is only the inadequacy of language, coupled with the shortcomings of rational consciousness, that caused the Ari to describe the information that was channeled through him, in words, which seem to indicate that metaphysical activities evolve in terms of time, space and the linear form.

Therefore, the student of Kabbalah should be ever wary of words in Kabbalistic treatises which seem to imply space, time and motion. It is important to remind oneself of the two perspectives, finite and infinite, from which all Kabbalistic concepts must be viewed.

Only from the finite or so-called "rational" perspective, meaning as seen from the standpoint of this illusionary world, do words such as "time", "space", "upper", "lower", "above", "below", "ascent", "descent", "physical" and "metaphysical" have purpose and function. From the infinite perspective there are no distinctions, no differentiations, no time, no space, no restrictions of any kind. All that exists from the infinite point of view is cause and effect of different dimensions, various levels of consciousness.

The language of the rational world is indeed illusionary. However, the Ari was capable of transmitting the description of the reality realm through mundane words used in our illusionary world.

One of the greatest mysteries of life is, that the languages of even the most primitive peoples, languages that have never been reduced to writing, are extremely complex. How did these languages develop as they did?

Language is considered to have been formed during the prehistoric age among the human race. Yet, little is known about the various steps in its formation. Language now contains a great number of concepts which are suitable tools for more or less unambiguous communication about events in daily life.

These concepts were acquired gradually without critical analysis by using the language. After having used a word often, we think that we more or less know what it means. It is quite obvious that the words are not so clearly defined as they seem to be at first sight. Furthermore, they have a limited range of applicability.

For example, we can discuss a piece of iron or wood. However, we cannot speak about a piece of water. The word "piece" of course, does not apply to liquid substances. Another example: we enter a candy shop and ask for a dollar's worth of mixed candy. The shopowner takes two sweets and hands them to us and says, "here you have two sweets, you can do the mixing yourself." Obviously the word "mixed" was misunderstood. This intrinsic uncertainty of the meaning of words was noticed at its early beginnings which brought about the need for definitions. But even definitions can be stated only with the help of other concepts. In essence one will have to rely on some concepts that are taken as they are.

Then there is the language of physics. The language of physics confines itself to a description of those phenomena within its field of study. Even though physics claims for itself the crown of fundamental science, it makes no pretensions that its own language can fully describe nonscientific phenomena. The language that has developed in physics is their new way of viewing the world and seems at odds with the language we use in our everyday lives.

The physicist faces a dilemma. The advanced experimental

techniques of quantum mechanics bring into the scope of science new dimensions of nature. They cannot be described in their present terms. The question is, in what language could they or should they be described. The only language that emerged from the process of scientific clarification was the mathematical language.

Following on the heels of relativity, quantum mechanics and probability, the language of mathematics no longer served as a precise description of reality. Relativity and quantum have altered the way we view space and time. They have focused our attention on the inability of the language of classical physics to describe the phenomena of a four and possibly ten dimensional relativistic universe.

Science recognizes that the *observer* creates reality by the process — both physical and mental — of filtering out data. Furthermore, the study of science no longer can include the properties of nature but only our observation *about* nature. Thus, the indeterminate state has now become a property of the universe.

If, indeed, the universe is pervaded with an underlying essence — which Kabbalah claims — then that realm will always remain inaccessible to the observer due to the subjectivity of perception. Each observer projects his or her own consciousness. Sir James Jeans[69] went so far as to suggest that the image of the universe is dependent on its structuring by a pervasive cosmic consciousness. He maintained that our perception of reality comes more from the interactions of our minds and senses than from the existence of any fundamental truths or physical laws.

Subjectivity, or each individual's desire to receive, affects the perception of what is being observed. Consequently, how can one person describe through language what has been observed, when another observer will see it from another perspective. For example, three people notice a structure. One might call it a home, another a house and yet another might address it as a building. Quite obviously, the one using the word "home" has seen it from his or her state of consciousness at that moment.

The inaccuracy and ambiguity of language may be helpful to poets who work largely with the subconscious. Science on the other hand, strives for unambiguous associations and for clear definition. The scientific method of abstraction is very efficient and powerful, but there is a price tag for it.

When taking a picture, the more accurately we focus on the object, the clearer it becomes. But we sacrifice for this clarity the whole of the surroundings. We now see the tree but no longer the forest. As we define our concepts more precisely, as we simplify them and mark the connections more and more exactly, it becomes increasingly detached from the real, quantum world.

Werner Heisenberg, the famous physicist, held this notion of language when he stated, "The problems of language here are really serious. We wish to speak in some way about the structure of the atoms, but we cannot speak about atoms in ordinary language."

The study of the atom compelled physicists to realize that language is completely inadequate to describe the atomic and subatomic reality. As we penetrate deeper and deeper into nature, we have to abandon more and more of the concepts of ordinary language.

On the journey to the world of the infinitely small, the experience is not an ordinary one and not comparable to that of our daily environment. Knowledge about it cannot be derived from direct sensory experience or the five senses. Therefore, our ordinary language, which takes its images from the world of the five senses, is no longer adequate to describe the observed phenomena.

As we penetrate deeper and deeper into the world of reality, we find that particle intelligences are so minute, they tend to be almost nonexistent or possibly even are a wave consciousness. Like the Kabbalists, physicists now have a glimpse, without the use of the five senses, of the true reality realm, the world of consciousness. How does one create a language to describe such concealed phenomena?

This was a task left for the Ari, Rabbi Isaac Luria, whose vision of the world of consciousness, the realm of hidden phenomena was as clear to him as the physical reality is completely visible to us. Many are still of the opinion that all the words and names in Kabbalah are of an abstract nature. They believe this since Kabbalah is involved with the Lightforce and spirituality.

The concepts dealt with in Kabbalah are beyond the field of time, space and motion, and even the imagination cannot grasp them. Not only is it beyond time, but the exact opposite is true. Kabbalah makes use of names and attributes only for their realistic and practical value. One of the fundamental rules among Kabbalists is that we cannot define that which we cannot conceive.

In the physical world of our senses, there are tangible things whose *essence* we neither understand nor imagine. Take for example electricity or magnetism. Who would say that the names used for these items are not real? We fully recognize how they work, and for the most part, we're not really concerned that we have no comprehension of their essence, namely the electron itself. Yet the name is very real and close to us. It appears as if we fully understand it. Even little children recognize the name "electricity" just as they easily recognize the words "bread" and "sugar."

The same is true with all terrestrial and celestial creatures. All that we recognize in this world, including our friends and relatives, is nothing more than a recognition of the effects that develop when our senses interact with them. The limited vision of our understanding is sufficient for us despite our inability to seize the nature or meaning of the essence. Moreover, some or many of us cannot comprehend even our own essence. We seem to have lost touch with ourselves. All that we know or can tell about our own essence is based on the results and outcome of our actions, and yet, we are very real and close to ourselves. We recognize our faults and attributes without necessarily understanding our essence.

The names and expressions appearing in Kabbalistic works are real and tangible. Although there may be no comprehension of their essence or meaning, nevertheless those who utilize these Kabbalistic names and expressions fully and completely understand them in their entirety. Strictly speaking, they know the particulars and accomplishments resulting from the Lightforce with our comprehension of and interaction with It.

Taking this matter one step further, the subject of the Lord or Lightforce and the language needed to portray or provide a comprehension of Its essence or meaning becomes even more difficult, if not totally incomprehensible.

The recitation of the *Shema*[70] was part of the daily worship in the Holy Temple. Its importance may be judged from the fact that the sages ordained that it be recited in the synagogue service, and provided it a central place in the morning and evening prayers. A closer examination of the text of the *Shema* reveals yet another mystery in our quest for pure language.

"And you shall *love* the Lord, your Lord." Performing a scriptural commandment of love for the Lord appears beyond even the rationale of dogma. Firstly, how does one comprehend being coerced into loving something or someone? Secondly, how do we go about loving without a personal contact with the object of our love?

To understand the true meaning of "love" requires a flawless comprehension and definition of the concept of fear. The words of the Bible merely project, albeit in a concealed manner, through what is considered commandments or tales, true meanings of this perfect language known as Hebrew.

All religions foster the idea of fear of the Lord in one manner or another. And yet the idea of fear never really took hold within the hearts of its practitioners as evidenced by the incessant and continuing misbehavior of mankind. Then again, how can we possibly fear an entity that we have never come face to face with?

Before beginning our examination of these two concepts and their subsequent Kabbalistic definition, I would like to clarify the precept of *Mitzvah* that has been so misunderstood that it has brought about much confusion with the Biblical text in general and the Jewish religion in particular.

Upon closer examination of the Hebrew word *Mitzvah*, (a precept also translated as commandment), we discover that the root of this word originates from another word *Tzavat*[71] which means to join or connect. Consequently, the English translation of the word *Mitzvah* to mean commandment, is essentially a gross misunderstanding and corruption of the true intent and meaning.

To further accentuate the erroneous development of mankind's understanding as to what took place with the Revelation at Sinai, let us consider for a moment the Divine Proclamation known as the Decalogue, or the Ten Commandments.[72]

No religious document has exerted a greater influence on the major religions than the Decalogue.[73] These few brief "commands" — only 120 words in all — seem to set forth the fundamental moral and social rules for all mankind. The Revelation at Sinai was heard not by Israel alone, but by the inhabitants of all the earth. The sound of the Lightforce divided itself into the 70 different languages spoken on earth,[74] so that all peoples might understand its eternal message.

As the Decalogue rang out, the dead were revived and took themselves to Sinai.[75] Even the souls of all the unborn generations were assembled there.[76] As the Divine "Commandments" rang out from Sinai, no bird sang, no ox bellowed, the ocean did not roar and no creature stirred.

From the above came the misguided conclusion that all of nature was entranced in breathless silence at the sound of the Divine voice, fearful, stunned and frozen in their tracks. And how does one explain why unborn souls or the dead were so drawn to this momentous event which appeared as nothing more than a religious experience.

A further misleading interpretation of the Decalogue is the name placed upon this unforgettable moment in human history: The Ten Commandments. The original ten presentations are known by the Hebrew title *Aseret haDibrot*, the Ten Speakings or Utterances. Nowhere, neither in the Talmud nor the Zohar, is there ever a mention of Ten Commandments.

I shall now try to go a little deeper into the meaning of this theosophical conception of the Ten Commandments, which it can hardly be doubted, has exercised a decisive influence on the majority of Scriptural writers. It rests upon a basic assumption to which I have referred previously, where I tried to trace the origin of the mistaken idea that the "Lord commands."

Historically, Judaism has tended to carry the process of commandments even further, striving to detect successively new layers in the mystery of the Lord's intent when commanding and demanding obedience, surrender and subservience. The more the original perception of Divine reality was externalized and transformed into mere religiosity, in which the symbols lost their tremendous meaning and unfettered allegory filled their empty husks, the more did original thinkers among the Kabbalists strive to penetrate into new and yet deeper layers of Lightforce consciousness.

Stretching the matter of commandments to its extreme, the following discussion in the Zohar reveals for us a new, and for many, a bizarre interpretation of its essential meaning. However, I trust that the Zohar will correct our previously learned notion that Biblical and Divine intention falls into a framework of religion. Rather, as we shall discover, the Bible is more of a roadmap with marks that illuminate our journey along the path of life.

"And the Lord spoke unto Moses, saying: *command* Aaron and his sons."[77] The Hebrew word for command is *Tzav*, and one might agree that from the text, the translation, command, appears to correspond to the Biblical intent. However the Zohar,[78] in one of its most striking declarations departs from the conventional interpretation and pursues an entirely different and radical approach to the Biblical intent of *Tzav*.

And therefore the other side [negativity of the Dark Lord] has been given to and placed in the hands of the Priest, as it is written, "*Tzav* Aaron and his sons saying...." There is a deep secret here, as we have already explained. That when the word *Tzav* appears in the Biblical text, it refers to idol worshipping, the other side, and in this verse, it was given over to him (the Priest) to burn this evil thought and to remove it from the holy intent which through sacrifices ascends upwards on high. And the *Tzav*, which is the other side, is given over to the priest to separate the other side from the holy by the various sacrifices.

And if you raise the question, how could the verse also make use of the word *Tzav* when addressing the people of Israel, since the Israelites do not have the same supernal powers to sever the Dark Lord from themselves, the Zohar responds that, when Israel follows the path of the Lightforce and connects with its energy, then the other side has no dominion over them.[79]

This particular Zohar stresses the contention of the Kabbalist that Biblical precepts were more a code awaiting decoding than the mere establishment of organized religion. What seems to emerge from the Zohar is the startling revelation that the Hebrew word for commandment, *Tzav*, is nothing more than a code name for the Dark Lord.

Furthermore, why, one may ask, did the Biblical text choose the word *Tzav* (command) to represent the code name for the Dark Lord? Any other word in the Hebrew language certainly would have sufficed to be used for this purpose.

The message set forth in the preceding Zohar some two

thousand years ago already foresaw the direction established religions would take in the future. The original intent of Revelation on Mount Sinai was misinterpreted. Originally the revealing of the Lightforce in our mundane terrestrial realm, together with a precise system (the Ten Sayings) permitted mankind to draw the awesome power of the Lightforce into their daily lives. Thereby it creates a security shield, and thus, prevents chaos and disorder, the trademark of universal existence.

A preoccupation of most religionists is whether one obeys or disobeys the word of the Lord. The relationship between the Deity and man is seen as one of a Lord and his servant. The Bible is the manual on subserviency.

The Zohar, following its interpretation of *Tzav*, understood that revelation on Mount Sinai and its significance did not reflect a religion consisting of commandments. Worship, or dedication in the service of the Lord were hollow terms. Over the centuries, this sort of belief has not brought the peoples of the world any closer towards their objective of world peace.

What has emerged from all this turmoil is the inadequacy of all religions to make manifest their doctrine or hopes among the majority of earth's inhabitants. There is no communication or common language between them.

Revelation on Mount Sinai revealed the Ten Channels of Communication between man and the Lightforce. Mastery over one's destiny now became accessible to all of mankind. The freedom of exercise, the choice of connecting with the Lightforce, remained, as always, with mankind. The doctrine of "no coercion in spirituality" was not disturbed with Revelation.[80]

To provide an insight into the awesome power of the

Lightforce and Its beneficence, the Sages furnished several descriptions by which the limited, logical and rational mind may grasp its profundity. The idea that "the souls of all the unborn generations were assembled there," pointed up the *infinite* consciousness of the Lightforce. Unborn is merely a term or definition that we mortals associate with time, namely, before, now and after.

Unlike the body, the soul is not subject to the space/time paradigm of past, present and future. The soul has access to the quantum consciousness of the Lightforce, where past, present and future exist in a single all-inclusive multidimensional plane.

The future is for the soul to behold. There is no reason why we can't see the future or remember the past. They are equally fixed and invariable. Connection to the Lightforce makes manifest within ourselves this beneficence.[81]

"The dead were revived and took themselves to Sinai," reflects the eternal characteristic of the Lightforce. Death is a concept placed in *our* illusionary reality of the world. On Mount Sinai the illusionary realm of concealment was removed, thereby revealing what already existed all along, and in the first place.

What is more important, and particularly addressing ourselves to the subject matter of this chapter — language, is that the Sages of the Talmud stated with regard to this phenomenon that "the sound of the Lightforce divided itself into 70 different languages spoken on earth." This idea may well be the most profound concept which we mortals, with our limited perspective of reality, may ever comprehend prior to the full revealment of the Lightforce. The actual coming of the Messiah, where the collective consciousness of all mankind will be connected with the Tree of Light reality, will contribute to a model of the grand unification of all mankind.

No longer will the cosmos and man, the inanimate and the animate, be understood as isolated entities, but rather as integrated elements. It is not one individual that brings the Messiah. The Ari, in his elevated state of consciousness could have brought the realm of Messiah. However, it required the participation of his students. He could not do it alone. When the collective consciousness of all mankind is brought together, and a pure awareness of the intrinsic wholeness of reality is achieved, then, and only then, has mankind been restored to the state of revelation.

Let us now return to the phenomenon of language and its relationship to Revelation on Mount Sinai. A good starting point for our examination is the question, why and where did the 70 languages originate?

"...AND THE WHOLE EARTH WAS OF ONE LANGUAGE AND ONE SPEECH"[82] Rabbi Shimon began his discussion with the verse: "for the house [the holy Temple], in its being built was built of stone made ready at the quarry; and there was neither hammer nor ax nor any tool of iron heard in the house while it was in building."[83] The phrase "in its being built" implies self-building, as though without the hands of artisans... In reality it was made of itself, by a miracle. So soon as the artisans set their hands to the work, it showed them [the hands] how to proceed in a manner quite novel to them, the reason being that the Lightforce rested on their hands, and similarly here, in the building of the Temple. It was built of its own accord, though seemingly by the hands of the laborers. The Lightforce showed the workers a design which guided their hands and from which they did not turn their eyes until the whole building of the house was completed.[84]

...When the Lightforce wills that Its light be revealed, there issues forth from His thought a determination that it should spread forth; whereupon it spreads from the undiscoverable region of thought until it rests in *garon* (throat), a spot in which perennially flows the Force of the *Spirit of Life.*

When the thought, after its expansion, comes to rest in that place, it is called *Elohim Hayyim* (living Lord). It then seeks to spread and reveal itself further, and there comes forth from this region fire, air and water, all compounded together [as three unified columns of left, central and right intelligences] referred to by the code name of Jacob, which brings forth sound or voice and becomes audible.

Thus the thought that was hitherto undisclosed and withdrawn in itself is now revealed through sound. In the further extension and disclosure of the thought, the voice strikes against the lips, and thus comes forth speech which is the culmination of the whole and in which the thought is completely revealed.

"... And there was neither hammer nor ax nor any tool of iron." This alludes to the world of illusionary reality, which depends upon the Thought [Lightforce consciousness] and is not heard or admitted inside when the Thought ascends on high to draw fresh sustenance. [The world of illusion does not place its stamp of limited influence on the Thought process].

When the Thought so expresses Itself, all of them rejoice and draw sustenance and are filled with blessings. At that time *all worlds* are sustained as one unity without any division whatsoever. After they have taken their respective portions they all disperse each to its side and to its assigned function.

Hence the Scripture states, "And the whole earth was of one language," the lips were combined as one, unified whole, the upper worlds (upper lip) and lower worlds (lower lip) acted and expressed the unity of all the worlds. Therefore, "and of one speech," there was no separation in the worlds and all existed within the mystery of oneness and integration.

And the verse continues, "and it came to pass as they journeyed *miquedem*" (lit. from before),[85] i.e., they journeyed away from that which is the starting point of the world [which prohibited the drawing of light from above to oneself alone], "and they found a valley in the land of Shin'ar," for from there spreads out the force and power of separation [the force and power of harsh judgment] there lies the source of uncertainty and chaos [known as the *Klippah* of Babel].

So it is written of Nimrod: "And the beginning of his kingdom was Babel," this being the starting point from which Nimrod began to attach himself to the power of the other side [to the force of the Dark Lord, chaos and uncertainty, and to swing away from the Lightforce, structure and certainty]. Similarly here "they found a valley in the land of Shin'ar," a place in which they conceived the idea of forsaking the Lightforce for another power.[86]

"And the Lord said: behold they are one people, and they have all one language![87] Being united they may well succeed in their undertaking. Come let us go down, and there confound their language, that they may not understand one another's speech. And the Lord scattered them abroad from there upon the face of all the earth. And they ceased to build the city."

Why was their language confounded? Because they all spoke Hebrew, and this was of help to them. For when they spoke and prayed, the Hebrew words fully expressed the inner intentions of the heart and mind and thus assist the people to the attainment of their goal. Hence, their language was confounded in order that they may not be able to express their metaphysical thoughts and intentions of the heart.

Since the angels, the carriers of metaphysical intelligences and dispatches *do not* understand any language save Hebrew, therefore as soon as the language of the rebels against the Lightforce was confounded, they lost the system to tap the source of their awesome power.

Whatever men utter below in Hebrew, all the hosts and Channels of heaven understand and take heed. Any other language they do not understand.

Hence, as soon as the language of the builders was confounded, they discontinued their efforts to build the city; since their strength was broken, and they were unable to achieve their purpose.[88]

In this revealing section of the Zohar, a key element of the Zoharic world view, one might almost say the essence of it, is the idea of assisting all of mankind toward an awareness of the unity and mutual interconnectedness of all aspects and events. It, therefore, comes as no surprise when the Zohar declares that Hebrew was the universal language for earth's inhabitants. There is no way in which world harmony can become a reality without a means of communication among all people.

The idea that Hebrew is the language exclusively for the Jewish people is, from a Zoharic viewpoint, a misconception of its inherent purpose. The objective of Hebrew is, to provide our thought consciousness with an opportunity to reveal itself, without the usual confusions that create different versions as to what is being said. A lecturer may share his thoughts, and yet, what the students hear may differ from the lecturer's thoughts.

It is for this reason that the Zohar describes precisely how our thoughts ultimately become manifested in the spoken word. Truly dramatic, this incredible insight into the procedure of thought connecting itself into the spoken word is something for the most part we have accepted without giving this matter much thought.

Indeed, how can a thought instantaneously become converted into a voice-word manifestation? The process, while unaffected by our space/time frame, seems to be completely robotic without our paying too much attention to the final word or sentence.

Language, therefore, involves more than merely a voice-word expression of thought. How the thought emerges will largely depend on the central activity of the person making the remark. Thought or flashes of the mind originate with the Lightforce. When thought flows and comes forth from the region of Jacob[89], central column, as three unified columns of left, central and right intelligences, the thought or Lightforce will then express itself without any admixture or interference of negative energy-intelligences that may be present at the time of its utterance. Mind and mouth are then in complete harmony with each other. It is precisely for this reason that when the thought finally expresses itself, the listeners will, in all probability, hear the same idea. A single all-pervasive force is the motivation and sustaining influence of all existence, physical and metaphysical, illusionary and real. Only the illusionary aspect of existence creates a state of confounding languages or thoughts.

The real aspect, the Lightforce, is constant, eternal and always remains in a unified state of intelligence. Consequently, when the Lightforce or thought moves through its stages of emanation, there is an aspect of unification within the atmosphere, within us, within everything that exists in this world.

By the same token, King Solomon, when building the Temple, had no need for hammer or ax. Material, physical entities are no longer realities when the Lightforce is tapped into and reigns dominant. The illusion of corporeality falls by the wayside and does not leave its imprint.

Physicists today provide a glimpse into the future, and the behavior of the corporeal illusionary realm of existence. They conclude that in theory we should have the ability to walk through closed doors and walls. Eugene Wigner, famous American physicist, held, that the universe could not really exist if there were no one here to observe it. John Wheeler, another physicist stressed that no phenomenon is a phenomenon until it is a registered phenomenon. He would say that we must, therefore, accept the fact that reality is dependent upon the existence of consciousness.

Conceivably, if our consciousness is directed towards the idea that the door or wall does not exist, then in reality, it does not.

The real problem lies in the fact that we are too material-conscious to achieve an altered state of mind over matter, and thus, cannot immaterialize the illusionary reality of the world around us.

An altered state of mind over matter corresponds to a predominance of the Lightforce. It then makes its presence felt over all limitations that emerge from the illusionary reality of our physically dominated world of existence. The Lightforce, when permitted to retain its rulership, vaporizes and literally eliminates chaos, disorder, pain and misfortune, the trademark of the Tree of Knowledge reality of our physically manifested universe.

The reader may have taken notice of my wording "when permitted" in the previous paragraph. How can we address the Lightforce and imply that somehow we direct, manipulate or even control the movement and desire of the Lightforce. Some may even consider this kind of thinking as outright heresy. If indeed the Lightforce is omnipotent then the power of an omnipotent Lord is without limit.

Omnipotence, however raises some awkward theological questions. Is the Lightforce of the Lord free to prevent evil? If yes, then why does It fail to do so?

This devastating analysis becomes more acute when we consider evil. If evil in the world is from the intention of the Lightforce, then It is not benevolent. If evil is contrary to Its intention, then It is not omnipotent. If evil depends completely on human activity because the Lord has given us free will, still when He doesn't prevent us from doing evil, must He not share some responsibility for not doing so?

Furthermore, if the Lord already knows the future, what meaning can we attach to our participation in it? An infinite

Lightforce will know what is happening all the time and everywhere.

As discussed in a previous chapter the idea of multiple realities is our only solution to the problem of free will versus determinism. Consequently, while the future is already known as to the outcome of the two realities of Tree of Life and Tree of Knowledge, free will permits mankind to choose either reality. But then one may still question as to whether one has a free choice in choosing either reality if the future is already known and is included as part of the present and past time frame.

Does one really have free will to choose one reality over another? Who in their right *mind* would even consider the chaotic reality of Tree of Knowledge? This is precisely the point made by the Kabbalist. Born with an active consciousness of only four percent, most of us fail even to recognize the possibility of altering our state of consciousness.

The Lightforce, governed by the doctrine of Bread of Shame, remains aloof and divorced from the Tree of Knowledge reality. Furthermore, there is no such reality as the illusionary reality of Tree of Knowledge, consequently, how could the Lightforce possibly invade or intervene within this reality, since it is our own observation of this reality that creates the illusion of its existence.

Isn't this the same notion as that of Wheeler and Wigner, previously mentioned? This illusionary realm exercises an overwhelming influence over our four percent mind. This prevents most of us from entertaining the idea that we physically exist in a world of illusion. All depends upon which mind frequency we operate: the limited four percent or an altered state of consciousness connected with the certainty, benevolent reality of the Lightforce.

Mankind's free will is the ability to remove the many evils that conceal the Lightforce. The Force has never ceased in its illumination. Obstruction to its beneficence was a normal consequence of the Bread of Shame doctrine. To share in and connect with the certainty and benefits of the Lightforce required knowledge and Kabbalistic information on how to illuminate the road of life's journey.

With each veil removed, the path becomes clearer, ever more certain. That which heretofore were obstacles that could not be observed, are now revealed and so we merely steer ourselves clear of them.

As the Lightforce makes its presence apparent, the marks and signs along our life trip become abundantly clearer. Try to compare this idea to a grand ballroom where lights are connected to a dimmer device. As we illuminate the ballroom we begin to observe more of the contents of the room. Once the full expression of the light has been achieved, then nothing previously concealed remains a mystery for us.

When the ballroom was dark, we imagined many items that may or may not have been present in the room. Once all elements of concealment were lifted, uncertainty disappeared. As the veils are lifted, the Lightforce itself, never diminished in Its intensity or brilliance, shines once again.

The notion that we put lights *on* in a dark room is an illusionary concept. The light is ever present. We cannot, because of the creative process, observe the light at its inception. We must earn its brilliance and beneficence. Therefore, imaginary, illusionary coverings or veils have been placed over the Lightforce, providing mankind with an opportunity to earn its beneficence of certainty and complete fulfillment.

The language of Kabbalah is the system of removing these layers. Like an onion made up of layer upon layer, sound and script impose upon the primal oneness their layers of concealment.

Observed externally every layer and detail stands by itself. But when man removes these layers, then there shines upon us the cosmic light of the world of unity where everyone and everything is combined into a oneness. In this essential binding union, there are no differentiations, whether they be personalities or languages.

It is the basic function of mankind to recognize that the pure light is, due to the doctrine of Bread of Shame, too strong for the world to endure. The Lightforce must be earned. Yet, it must illuminate the world, if we are to achieve *Gmar haTikune*, the complete correction.

It is necessary that there be many curtains or veils to soften the Lightforce, and these veils are what constitute the element of chaos and uncertainty. The difficulty lies with our limited perception of the Lightforce hidden behind these illusionary, removable obstructions. Somehow we have lost the ability to perceive that all chaos is but a veil necessary in order to provide us with an opportunity to earn our bread. These veils permit a free will decision to adjust the flow of light at our discretion.

The language of Kabbalah pierces right through the layers of speech and sound. It touches at the very heart of the Lightforce. Through a complex web of interacting angels, the Hebrew language permits all of mankind to return to the former times of the Tower of Babel. However, this time around, we shall have learned our lesson. The purpose of our presence is to restore the Lightforce in its full splendor. Pursuing the Dark Lord has been and continues to remain an exercise in futility.

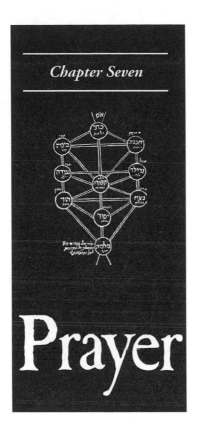

Chapter Seven

Prayer

THE LANGUAGE OF KABBALAH PROVIDES THE QUANTUM effect that prayer originally responded to. Of all human activity there is nothing so inclusive to man as prayer. It is one of the few activities of man that has no counterpart in the animal world, for only man was destined to rule over the entire universe and all that is contained within it.

As with everything in the coded text of the Bible, the central message is packaged with others. Witness Adam's first assigned task in the Garden of Eden:[90] "And out of the ground the Lord formed every beast of the field, and every fowl of the air; and brought them unto Adam to see what he would call them; and whatsoever Adam called every living creature that was the name thereof."

The exercise was designed to do far more than keep

Adam occupied and insulate him from ennui. Of all the fears that bedevil mankind, none is so terrifying as fear of the unknown; what is unknown can neither be avoided nor controlled. By naming the creatures of a newly formed world, Adam became the master of his environment. According to the Zohar, Adam was the first and only human at the time of Creation with the ability to control the vast universe.[91] However, he was not the last of his line to wield the power of a name.[92]

The Zohar abounds with references to the role of man in achieving mastery of his destiny. As portrayed by the Zohar, man is a spiritual entity whose fate is determined by his thoughts and actions. Rather than a rigid adherence to dogmatic doctrine, Kabbalah places prayer in the context of spiritual experience.

Genesis[93] declares that man was created on the sixth day of the Lord's creative process.[94] Why, asks the Zohar, was the creation of man saved for last? Because he is the culmination of all that preceded. In addition to being mere participants in the cosmic scheme, man, according the Zohar, was given the role of determiner of universal and galactic activity.

The Zohar[95] reveals the dynamic interplay and interconnectedness of our universe and man's relationship to it:

> For there is not a member in the human body that does not have its counterpart in the world as a whole. For as man's body consists of members and parts of various ranks, all acting and reacting upon each other so as to form one organism, so does the world at large consist of a hierarchy of created things, which when they properly act and react upon each other form one organic body.

The preceding Zohar stresses the intimate connection between the celestial kingdom and our mundane realm. As seen by the Zohar, the human body is a reflection of the vast cosmos. Human organs and limbs mirror the dynamics of an interstellar dance that is ever present in the universe.

The Zohar predicts that all inhabitants of planet Earth will one day come to grips with the profound mysteries of our cosmos and the many problems confronting mankind. No longer will man be forced to bow to the wisdom of experts, scientists and authorities who live in a rarified intellectual atmosphere, beyond the reach of the mainstream of humanity. In that time which has become known as the Age of Aquarius, the individual will again seize control of his sense of wonder and inquisitiveness, and, thus armed, regain a thorough knowledge of the exact nature of the universe and each person's place in it.

Prayer, or the language of Kabbalah, is a "Jacob's ladder"[96] combining and connecting earth to the celestial realm. Most people are initially surprised to discover the significant role prayer plays in the Biblical text. For the most part, prayer or meditation is often used to beseech the assistance and support of the Lord when one is troubled, or to express thanksgiving when the Lord responds and fulfills our needs.

From a Kabbalistic point of view, however, the concept of prayer as it is expressed in the Biblical text takes on a completely different and even opposite role. Instead of concentrating on the plain meaning of the prayers, the Kabbalist dwells in the realm of the Divine forces and when reciting the words, directs his mind to the Lightforce which governs and motivates every living force.

The doctrine of *Kavanah*, which is the meditation that accompanies the words of prayer, is primary, whereas the words themselves are considered secondary in importance. The Kabbalist considers the words as the body or channel for the more important phase of *Kavanot* which I liken to the soul of prayer.

Bahya ibn Paquda remarks that prayer without concentration, or *Kavanot*, is like a body without a soul, or a husk without a kernel.[97] The word *Kavanah* stems from the word *Kivune*, direction, indicating that the mind must take a direction when reciting prayers. As to the word prayer, the Hebrew word most commonly used is *Tefillah*,[98] the root of which means trivial, or secondary.

These meanings are eminently suited to the Kabbalistic conception of prayer as being a means of control leading to the opportunity of becoming the master of one's destiny. Prayer, then, is the communication system by which man fulfills the original intent and purpose of his existence as determined in Genesis, as previously mentioned.

The spiritual essence of the Hebrew Aleph Beth emanates from the highest realms of the *Sfirot*, the energy packets of the Lightforce of the Lord. The Aleph Beth and the words that are formed from it are permeated with the spirit of the Creator, and thus, sealed with the Impression of His Signature, which is Truth.

To whom is the Lord close? This question is posed in the Zohar regarding the words, "The Lord is near to those who call upon Him."[99] The answer is: "To those who call upon Me in Truth." The Zohar asks, "Is there anyone who would call falsely?" Rabbi Abba said, "Yes. It is the one who calls (prays) and knows not Whom he calls."

The Zohar raises and answers yet another question:

"What is the meaning of the word *Emeth* [Truth]? The answer is: It is the seal and connection to the Lightforce."[100] Truth then embodies the Lightforce of the Lord. Truth is not relative, nor dependent upon which opinion carries *more* weight. Truth is not merely an aspect of our morality code demanding that we always tell the truth.

The "Ten-Commandment" prohibition of "Do not bear false witness"[101] means that when we lie, we are severed from the Lightforce. The following spectacular Zohar reveals the essential idea of truth as stated by the Psalmist, King David.

> A difference of opinion that was composed on the pattern of the supernal dispute, that created more and not less affinity between the disputants as the dispute continued, was that between Shammai and Hillel. The Lord approved of their dispute, for the reason that its motive was spiritual and that it therefore resembled the Lightforce which combined the right (imparting) and left (receiving) columns to achieve a circuitry and thus establish continuity similar to that which took place at Creation.[102]

Rabbi Ashlag explains that the preceding Zohar describes the Lightforce system in our universe. There was created: on days one and four the negative energy-intelligence (Desire to Receive); on days two and five the positive energy-intelligence (Desire to Share); on days three and six the process of Restriction[103] to give the human race the opportunity to remove Bread of Shame.

Consequently, the behavior of man on the terrestrial level could combine and unify this terrestrial level with the celestial level of the cosmos and, thus, provide stability, tranquility and peace on earth. This was the dispute between Shammai and Hillel. Shammai's internal nature originated from the left, or negative aspect of Creation, and therefore, his conclusions usually embodied the prohibitive or negative aspect of the Law. Hillel, contrarily, stemmed from the energy-intelligence of the right column, and consequently, provided a more affirmative approach to the Law.

Each, however, proceeded with their individual point of view from the perspective of the central column of restriction. Thus, they combined to establish a circuitry of energy within both realms of our universe. Their purpose and intent was solely for the ultimate unity of the different energy-intelligences, thereby to make the presence of the Lightforce felt throughout the universe and become manifest within all of mankind.

The opinions of Shammai and Hillel were not presented to dispute the other's opinions or to convince the other to adopt their own individual convictions. Rather, their disagreements were understood to be two different perspectives of the same essential whole, the Lightforce.

They recognized the individuality of all things to be equal, but, at the same time, they were aware that their differ-

ences and contrasts were essential within the all-embracing unity of the Lightforce. While for most people, differences of opinion will usually result in conflict and even terrible warfare, for Shammai and Hillel this was not so. Most of mankind finds it extremely difficult to accept the unity of contrasts or even the unity of opposites.

This is primarily due to the usual state of consciousness in which most of us exist. Once, however, an effort is made to transcend the material, corporeal realm in the pursuit of spirituality, we can become aware of the polar relationships of opposites. We have not found any difficulty with the light bulb, for example. We have come to realize that right or left are not absolute manifestations belonging to different categories. The two poles are merely two sides of the same reality, extreme parts of the single bulb.

The essential idea in Kabbalah is to transcend the familiar world of opposites, as Shammai and Hillel did. They were not limited to, or by, the emotional limitations and intellectual-rational disputations that are the underlying causes of strife, chaos and suffering in our mundane existence. Shammai and Hillel came to realize the elevated-spiritual realm of the unitive Lightforce.

This fundamental unity of the Lightforce is the basis of the unification of the opposite forces brought into our terrestrial realm by the phenomenon of Creation. When the Talmud provides us with the expression "This and its opposite are both the word of the Lord,"[104] essentially they furnish us with the idea of complimentarity. The picture as presented by Shammai and the viewpoint expressed by Hillel are two complimentary descriptions of the same reality, each providing a limited range of application to the essential whole, each furnishing a partial viewpoint in achieving a full description and understanding of the totality of any given reality or subject.

This then is *Truth*; an idea, notion or activity containing the fundamental reality of the Lightforce. This is the essential idea of prayer. To "call upon Him in Truth" refers to our ability to transcend the illusion-rational realm of existence and connect with the Infinite.[105]

Thus, the symbol of Jacob's ladder[106] represents and suggests prayer as a ladder by which mankind may link the celestial and terrestrial spheres with the Angels being the intermediaries, as it were, carrying messages one to the other. Unfortunately, states the Zohar, "most people who pray in their house of worship walk out empty".[107] Their prayers are recited in a robotic state of consciousness, devoid of any conscious meditative state of *Kavanot*. Truth is then absent, despite the recitation of each and every word of the prayer.

"Prayer should be offered with proper *Kavanah* on the words uttered in the Lord's presence."[108] "Rabbi Eliezer said: He that makes his prayer a fixed task, his prayer is not a prayer."[109] "Rabbi Shimon ben Nethaniel said: when you pray, make not your prayer a fixed form."[110] "A person who has just returned from a journey and is consequently unable to concentrate [*Kavanah*] properly, should not pray until three days have elapsed."[111]

What seems to emerge from the preceding talmudical passages is that the words by and within themselves do not serve the essential purpose of prayer. Without the proper meditation for any particular prayer, the words of prayer fall short of the target.

According to the Zohar, *Kavanah*, the directed-meditation

system is a significant as well as an integral element for spiritual growth.

> They said further that all depends on the kind of speech, action, and *Kavanah* to which a man habituates himself, for he draws to himself here below from on high that side to which he habitually cleaves. I found also in the same book the rites and ceremonies pertaining to the functions of the planets and signs of the constellations, and the directions for concentrating the thought upon them so as to draw them nearer to the worshipper. The same principle applies to him who seeks to be attached to the sacred spirit on high. For it is by his fervor and devotion [*Kavanah*] that he can draw to himself that spirit from on high.[112]

What emerges from the preceding Zohar is, that prayer is something more than merely a method or device by which we express our gratitude to the Lord for the beneficence that He sheds upon us. It involves man's participation in the quantum dynamics of the cosmos where fragmentation of our universe is once again to be restored to its original unity.

In another section of the Zohar, we find that the recitation of the words themselves is not to be considered as fulfilling or accomplishing the objective of prayer, as is clearly stated in the following excerpt:

> Prayer is made up of both action [phylacteries, tallit, standing, sitting and other prerequisites] and speech, and when the action is faulty, speech does not find a spot to rest in; such prayer is not prayer, and the man offering it is defective in the

upper world and the lower.[113]

Another Zohar clearly indicates the power and importance of prayer and teaches that prayer is anything but a matter of obedience, a form of request for assistance or an expression of thanksgiving:

> Come and see! Every day a proclamation goes forth [energy-intelligent consciousness], saying, "O ye peoples, this thing depends on your own effort." And this is the sense of the words, "Take ye from among you an offering unto the Lord," not as a burden, but "whosoever is of a willing heart let him bring the Shekhinah." From this we learn that prayer offered with concentrated devotion (*Kavanah*) by a man that fears his Master produces great effects on high, as already said elsewhere.[114]

Prayer is anything but a robotic instrument for alleviating the hearts of the saddened and the conscience of the evildoer. Our very lives and environment depend on this very powerful instrument to achieve control over our destinies. The hostile environment, the threatening cosmos, the natural enemies of our physical body, the degenerative process of aging — all represent the trials and tribulations that each of us faces every day.

Life, as a human experience, portrays a picture of chaos and suffering, from the first day that we breathe life into our physical system. For many, this struggle may begin in our mothers womb. No matter when it starts, the bottom line reads like a broken record: chaos, misfortune, and more of the same tomorrow. Somehow, despite our reverence and belief in prayer, nothing has really changed.

It, therefore, should come as no surprise that most of earth's inhabitants no longer include prayer as part of their daily routine. The time-honored ritual of prayer has not retained its magic spell for most religions. And yet, prayer with *Kavanah* as practiced by our Centres all over the globe has drawn tens of thousands to its practice, despite their inability to understand its meaning or, for that matter, even to be capable of reading the words. For the majority of its adherents, *scanning* has more than sufficed for them to experience the effect of prayer. No doubt, the added ingredient of *Kavanah* changed the feeling from that of robotic-obedience to one of connection with the Lightforce.

Another example provided by the Zohar[115], which stretches the significance of prayer to its extreme, is the lengthy discourse on the "prayers ascending on high."

> Rabbi Jose further discoursed on the verse: And he said unto me: "Thou art my servant, Israel, in whom I will be glorified."[116] Observe that in prayer by which a person must pray to the Lightforce, there is an outer, bodily connection with the Lightforce and an inner, spiritual connection, which is the essential true totality of prayer.

> The body possesses twelve members that participate in the outer, bodily connection with the Lightforce, [namely; two hands, two feet, each of which contain three segments making a total of twelve parts].

> Then there are the twelve internal members which are considered the spiritual aspect of the body, [namely: the brain, heart, liver, mouth,

tongue, five wings of the lung, and two kidneys]
whose act of connection with the Lightforce is of
benefit to the spirit. For this is the internal and
precious worship of the Lightforce, as expounded
among the mysteries taught by Rabbi Shimon,
and as belonging to the mysteries of supernal wisdom known to the Companions, praiseworthy is
their portion.

Prayer belongs to and is connected with the spirit.
Deep mysteries are attached to it. For mankind
does not know that a person's prayer splits and
penetrates the ethereal spaces, pierces the firmament, opens openings and ascends on high.

At the moment of daybreak, when the light
becomes separated from darkness, a proclamation
goes forth throughout all the firmaments, stating:
Prepare yourself, you guardians at the doors, you
sentinels of the Palace — each one to his post!

For the day-attendants are not the same as the
night-attendants, the two groups replacing each
other with the succession of day and night.

This secret is alluded to in the passage,"the greater
light (sun) to rule by day...and the lesser light to
rule by night"[117] indicating the day-attendants
and the night-attendants.... Each one, following
the proclamation, is assigned his suitable place.

The Shekhinah [the quantum, collective consciousness of the entire universe] then descends
and Israel enters the Synagogue to offer praise to

their Master in song and hymn. It behoves, then, every man, after equipping himself with the emblems of the outer, bodily connection [such as the fringes and phylacteries], to unify his heart and internal being for the act of worship and to say his prayers with devotion...

The angelic attendants all await the *proper* prayer to ascend to the ethereal realm. And if it is fitly uttered, all the chieftains kiss that utterance of prayer and carry it aloft into the supernal firmament where other chieftains await it. Then the letters of the Divine Name that abide in the ethereal space soar upwards.

That Divine Name is formed of twelve letters[118] and is the one by which Elijah literally flew to the ethereal regions until he reached heaven. The letters, then, of the Name fly upwards with the prayer-utterance, in company with the chief who holds the keys of the ether and all the other chiefs, until heaven is reached. Happy is the portion of the man who knows the proper way in which to structure his prayer.[119]

The power and significant consequences connected to and resulting from prayer as presented by the Zohar, are something we might expect to read in some science fiction novel or to appear on some movie screen as a first rate outer-space film. The discourse of the preceding Zohar does not seem to resemble or reflect the concept of prayer conventional religion proposes or postulates to its congregants.

The notion that prayer, when properly directed, can

provide mankind with the opportunity to fly in space will most certainly be dismissed if not rejected outright by most religious leaders. However considering the uselessness and futility of conventional prayer, our civilization can ill afford to reject the significance of *Kavanah.*

At this point I raise the question, how in the world do I expect so revolutionary a change as proposed by the Zohar, to become a working reality among the vast majority of prayer adherents and even those who have sworn off prayer as something they can very well do without in their desperate trip through the daily maze of difficulties?

The answer to this nagging question comes from our usual fountain and wellspring of timely information, the Book of Splendor, the Zohar. One of the many abstruse sections in the Zohar discusses repentance. Briefly stated, repentance as understood by the Zohar originates from the Hebrew word *Tshuvah,* which is comprised of two words or elements: *Tashuv Hei.* *Tashuv* means return. Return the *Hei* [final letter of the Tetragrammaton] restoring the Desire to Receive to one of also sharing.

The concern of the Zohar is that the concept of *Tshuvah* may mistakenly be understood to mean that one need only have a change of heart and all is forgiven.

Rabbi Eleazar said: all of the exiles that the Congregation of Israel experienced, the Lord placed a time limit as to when the banishment would end. For the final, present exile, no time or limit was established, for this entirely depends on *Tshuvah,* repentance, as stated in the Scriptures, "You shall return unto the Lord and you shall hearken unto his voice."[120] If your outcasts be at the utmost parts of heaven, from there will the Lord gather you and from there will He fetch you.[121]

Rabbi Akiva said, how can this come about, that the entire *world* will arouse themselves in *Tshuvah* all together. Those at the utmost parts of heaven, and those from the ends of earth, how will they join together and do *Tshuvah*?

Responded Rabbi Eleazar to Rabbi Akiva that, if the leaders of the synagogue return with *Tshuvah* in one synagogue, then the exile of all the peoples shall be brought to an end. For the Lord looks forward to the time when all shall return with *Tshuvah*.[122]

The response of Rabbi Eleazar raises an obvious question, how can the *Tshuvah* or Restoration of one synagogue bring about the final redemption of the entire world? By what process or phenomenon can the efforts of just a few affect the lives of all mankind reaching from one end of the earth to the other? Furthermore, why is it necessary that at least one entire synagogue return with *Tshuvah*? What force or power does this one synagogue create or bring about, so that the lives of all mankind become affected and in turn, restore the collective consciousness of the world?

Let us again dwell upon the Zoharic interpretation of repentance. That the concept of repentance implies the expression of regret or remorse for evil acts does not sit well with the Kabbalist. While the sinner may have found some relief or solace from his confession, or even promised to refrain from such acts in the future, what about the victim or the family that has been victimized?

Take an extreme violation of the moral code, the action of murder where the victim's family is left without any form of support for their daily sustenance. During the period of Repentance, while the murderer works his way through his *Tikune*, or correction, the family of the victim continues without bread on the table, not to speak of the emotional damage inflicted on the children who no longer enjoy or possess the support of the murdered parent.

Considering this essential flaw in Repentance, the Zohar examines the coded word for Repentance, and once deciphered, makes a great deal of sense. As stated previously, the word for repentance is *Tshuvah*, consisting of two aspects. *Tashuv* means return or restore and the Hebrew letter at the end of the word, the letter *Hei*, symbolizes the final letter of the Tetragrammaton.

Before we consider the following remarks of the Zohar, let us first examine the most sacred of all words in the Bible, the Tetragrammaton.[123] Various Hebrew names are used for the Lord in the Bible. Some of these are employed in both the generic and specific sense. Others are used only as the personal name of the Lord of Israel. The personal and most holy name of the Lord is written in the Hebrew Bible with four consonants YHVH and is referred to as the Tetragrammaton.[124]

The pronunciation of the name YHVH is avoided, and the word "Ad'nai" is substituted. In order to avoid pronouncing even the sacred name Ad'nai for YHVH, a custom was later introduced of saying simply in Hebrew *haShem* or simply the Name. The avoidance of pronouncing the name YHVH is generally ascribed to a sense of reverence.

However, reviewing the following Talmudical sources, one must conclude that reverence, or similar notion, is meaningless or an outright corruption of the essential idea behind the Names of the Lord. Firstly, from the point of view of rationale, are we to believe that the Lord is considered a member of the underworld and therefore found it necessary to adopt so many aliases to his real name. Secondly, the Talmud prohibits the pronunciation of the name of the Lord only as it applies to the Tetragrammaton, which could be pronounced by the high priest only once a year on the Day of Atonement in the Holy of Holies in the Temple.[125] The name was also pronounced by the other priests in the Temple when they recited the Priestly blessing.[126] The Talmud also expresses the prohibition as follows: "Not as I am written am I pronounced. I am written *Yud Hei Vav Hei* and I am pronounced *Aleph Dalet Nun Yud*."[127]

What seems to emerge from the Talmud is the idea that the Tetragrammaton represents an awesome channel for the Lightforce. Therefore its pronunciation or expression, which makes manifest the awesome power of the Lightforce exposes the individual to an overdose of the Lord's beneficence or Lightforce. If the person is ill-prepared to handle its energy the consequence would be disastrous. Consequently, a High Priest in the Holy of Holies on the Day of Atonement was insulated sufficiently to receive the total measure of beneficence for the entire world necessary to keep the universe in balance.

Therefore, the word *YHVH* is to be scanned only and pronounced as *Ad'nai*, which serves as a filter and reducing agent of the Lightforce. Following this brief description of the Tetragrammaton, and the use of its scanning consequences in the prayer book, the whole idea of prayers takes on new and awe-inspiring proportions. Prayer is one of the channeling systems for providing mankind with the benefits of the Lightforce, placing its adherents in a position of strength in overcoming the ever-present obstacles mankind faces each and every day.

Let us now consider the following profound Zohar which hopefully can clarify for us the apparent shortcomings concerning the conventional notion of Repentance and the Tetragrammaton in prayer.

> Rabbi Shimon said to Rabbi Elazar: Come and see. These twenty-two letters which are inscribed in the Bible are all expressed by the Ten Utterances [or Ten *Sfirot* — Crown, Wisdom, Intelligence, Mercy, Judgment, Beauty, Victory, Splendor, Foundation and Kingdom].[128] Each of these ten, which are the energy packets of the King's Lightforce, is traced in specific letters. [The letters are the secrets of the vessels of the *sfirot* and each *sfirah* has her special vessel]. Hence the Holy Name, the Tetragrammaton, is disguised in other letters [in *Ad'nai*, for the vessels of the coded realm *Z'eir Anpin*, the Tree of Life reality, which is the secret of the Tetragrammaton, and are disguised and enclothed in the vessels of *Malkhut* (Kingdom) which is the secret of *Ad'nai*].

> Each utterance lends to the one above it certain letters, so that they become included in one another. Therefore we trace or pattern the Tetragrammaton in other letters not its own, one set being concealed in the other, until they are all linked together.

> He who desires to know the combinations of the

holy names must know the letters which are inscribed in each crown and then combine them. I myself trace them from the profound book of Solomon, and so I am able to do it and reveal them to the Companions. sBlessed are the righteous in this world and the next, because the Lord desires to honor them and reveal to them profound secrets of the Holy Name [Tetragrammaton] which He does not reveal even to angels.

Thus Moses was able to sustain himself among the angels and they were not able to touch him, although they are like a burning flame and coals of fire. For if Moses did not possess the Holy Names how could he remain in their presence?

When Moses entered into the Cloud and came among the angels, an angel came upon Moses with flames of fire, flashing eyes and burning wings and sought to swallow him up. Kimel is his name. Then Moses mentioned a holy name inscribed within the twelve letters, the angel became confused and shaken until Moses left them.[129]

Included in the Centre's prayer book are the many and varied combinations of letters and *sfirot* mentioned in the preceding Zohar. We, who are witnesses to the Age of Aquarius are fortunate to be privy to Rabbi Isaac Luria's revelations concerning the matter of the Holy Names.[130] Those who lived prior to the age of Lurianic Kabbalah unfortunately were denied the privileged information. Rabbi Shimon stated in the Zohar that only with the appearance of the Age of Aquarius will the information concerning the Holy Names and other secret matters be revealed.

Moses' confrontation clearly demonstrates the awesome power of the Holy Names. Our prayer book, known as the prayer book of the Ari, Rabbi Isaac Luria, is essentially different from the standard, conventional prayer book inasmuch as it contains and includes the varied combination of letters. More importantly, the sfirotic vowels appear alongside the Holy Names indicating the particular *sfirah* concealed within the Holy Names.

The prayer book, then, represents more than a compendium of various thanksgiving or pleading incantations. Prayers, when properly expressed create the security shields such as the one Moses made use of in his encounter with the angels. If I were to trace the decline or lack of interest in prayer worship, I would most certainly attribute the central, if not major cause, to the ignorance of what prayer is all about.

The idea of prayer as being our connection to the Divine unfortunately does not, by itself, disclose its significance as a method or system to relieve the adversities of daily living with renewed strength and determination each day; the confidence generated by its awesome power and its effectiveness, as demonstrated by the results we shall experience.

The revelations of the Zohar, written some two thousand years ago, are making its presence felt again in our day. The joy and relief felt and expressed by individuals, many of whom are incapable of reading Hebrew fluently or understanding the meaning of the words, is an Aquarian phenomenon. Having faith and trust in ourselves that we are at least as capable as computer scanners, we permit the impressions to take over. Our perusing eyes, as they scan the Holy Names along with its sfirotic vowels, capture the internal, spiritual energy intelligences of the vowels and Holy Names, along with the other Hebrew letters that combine to produce the combination of Holy Names.

Whether our *four percent* rational consciousness comprehends the system, or why it works, is no longer important, as long as it does work. Those of us who refuse to release the grip of the insignificant *four percent*, deny ourselves access to the world of the *ninety-six percent* reality, and reject the quantum opportunity to tap the ineffable, quantum world of cosmic consciousness, the Tree of Life reality.[131] Our alter ego demands that we remain skeptics. Man's deadliest enemy, the ego, goads us into the belief that what the five senses cannot recognize or distinguish does not exist. It, therefore, comes as no surprise that individuals who have been programmed in the sciences, or follow Newtonian classical physics, find it extremely difficult to let go. Moreover, those who are accustomed to the act of prayer as a form of thanksgiving may find it likewise difficult to let go of their robotic system of prayer. And thus, the idea for change becomes something foreign to us.

With an idea of what the Tetragrammaton is all about, let us now investigate the Zoharic interpretation of *Tshuvah*, repentance, which, hopefully, will lead us to the elimination of a flawed concept.

The Biblical precept of Repentance is considered within the framework of the coded energy-intelligence *Binah*. And because of our misbehavior, when the Holy Temple was destroyed, we were left alone in the lower realm of *Malkhut* (Kingdom). And what is *Binah*? She originates from the letters *Bin* (son) *Yud Hei*. And *Bin* is the *Vav* of the Tetragrammaton which hints at the third letter of the Tetragrammaton or the

coded energy-intelligence of *Z'eir Anpin*, also
referred to by another code name *Tiferet.*[132] *Bin*
[son] *Yud Hei* also hints at the connection that
never ceases between *Tiferet* and *Yud Hei* sym-
bolizing the upper *sfirot* of *Binah* and *Hokhmah*.
And when one returns with *Tshuvah*, repentance,
it is as if he has returned or restored the realm of
Malkhut, which was severed due to misbehavior,
is again restored to its former connection with the
letter *Vav* and the Tetragrammaton is again
restored intact. The first three letters of the
Tetragrammaton — *Yud Hei Vav* now become
joined with the last *Hei*.[133]

This striking penetration of the mysteries that surround
the concept of *Tshuvah* leaves one with the awe-inspiring feeling
that there is more to religion than meets the eye; the idea that
what we are considering when *Tshuvah* takes place is a restoration
of our entire universe. The fact that simply saying "I'm sorry" has
very little bearing on future events comes as a shocking surprise.

Haven't we been taught since childhood that when we do
naughty things we should say "I'm sorry"? And yet we are not
educated to inquire as to how our verbalization of regret restores
or removes the pain and suffering we may have consciously or
unwittingly inflicted.

"I didn't mean it" or "I had no idea that what I had done
would cause such grief" are just a few of the expressions that provide the perpetrator with an easing of conscience. But, in fact, we
tend to ignore the consequences of our actions so long as "I am
sorry."

The idea of *Tshuvah*, states the Zohar, must go far

beyond a feeling of remorse. *Tshuvah*, as the Kabbalist understands this phenomenon, is the correction, restoration and undoing of the wrongdoing inflicted on others. The Hebrew word *Tshuvah* means returning to the original state or position prior to the action of severance.

Whenever one causes harm or unhappiness to others, the victim is severed or cut off from a previous state of contentment — relative, of course, to this particular action. This is not to say, that everyone is full of contentment and that this major or minor wrongdoing brought about discomfort and sorrow. What the Kabbalist is stating is that when one suffers at the hands of another, to the degree that this particular act has brought the victim additional or newly acquired unhappiness, the perpetrator must restore the sufferer to the previous condition.

Tshuvah, then, involves a "back to the future" concept. This phenomenon, according to the Kabbalist, is the vehicle by which the illusion of time, space and motion loses its control and influence. *Tshuvah* permits a forward and reverse situation when properly executed, thereby eliminating the severance and subsequent consequences of the hurt and suffering that normally accompanies acts of wrongdoing.

There have been many attempts, from a scientific point of view, to substantiate the feasibility and validity of this concept, but up to the present, to no avail. The Grandfather Paradox is what prevents the scientist from achieving a state of "back to the future." Mathematical formulae suggest two-way time travel, yet for the most part, the paradoxical consequences keep it within the framework of science fiction. Why?

The intent of this chapter is to establish the fact that two-way time travel is a Kabbalistic reality. How we avoid violating causality and overcoming the Grandfather Paradox is dealt with fully in my work *The Star Connection*.[134]

What is important, at this time, is to consider how prayer and two-way time travel may serve the process of *Tshuvah*. Let us now turn to another revealing Zohar concerning the *Tshuvah* phenomenon.

> Israel, return to the Lord; for thou hast stumbled in thy iniquity. Take with you *words*, and turn to the Lord, say to him: Forgive all iniquity, and receive us graciously so we will offer the *words* of our lips instead of calves.[135] The final *Hei* of the Tetragrammaton refers to the confessional *words*.

> For this is certain, that when man sins, the *Hei* becomes distanced from the *Vav* [of the Tetragrammaton]. The *Yud* (*Hokhmah*), *Hei* (*Binah*) and the *Vav* (*Tiferet*) become separated from the final letter *Hei* (*Malkhut*). A cosmic upheaval takes place [the Tetragrammaton represents the different levels of the cosmos, and when the Tetragrammaton becomes fragmented, then our cosmos is in disarray] and because of it, the Holy Temple was destroyed, and Israel was forced into exile from the Land of Israel.

> Consequently, those who achieve *Tshuvah* contribute to the restoration of the final *Hei* (*Malkhut*) following the letter *Vav*, and the collective redemption of mankind. Thus, everything depends upon *Tshuvah*. It has already been stated by the Sages, that all requirements for the final redemption have been completed. Redemption

now depends upon *Tshuvah*, the completion of His name. [For this is the secret of the final *Hei* completing the other three letters of the Tetragrammaton].

Therefore, it is stated in Scriptures, "And I acted for my name's sake."[136] Also "For my own sake, for my own sake will I do it [to defer anger][137] and if they do not return with *Tshuvah*, I [Lightforce] shall establish for them a king whose harsh decrees shall be more severe than those of Pharaoh. And the Israelites shall return with *Tshuvah* bereft of any other option.

But I wonder, since one causes evil to the world why does *Tshuvah* help? Assuredly, for one who does *Tshuvah* properly, returns the *Hei* to the *Vav*, *Tshuvah* restores everything, both above and below, restores himself and the entire world.[49]

What is clearly expressed by the Zohar, and the prophets Hosea and Isaiah is the significance, if not the centrality, of the Name of the Lord, the Tetragrammaton, in achieving a return and restoration of the past towards changing the future. The idea of being repentant, conscience-stricken and remorseful, is an important prerequisite in meeting the requirements towards achieving *Tshuvah*. The responsibility and obligation by the repentant never again to repeat the negative, or evil, activity is to be considered an essential component for restoration by *Tshuvah*. Nevertheless, omitting the Tetragrammaton and its meditative process or neglecting to include the *Kavanah*, mind-directed thought concerning the sfirotic vowel configuration, when reciting the particular prayer provided for *Tshuvah*, the requirements for complete restoration will not have been met.

And yet, for years the majority of worshipers with well-meaning intentions have realized that something is amiss. The result is empty synagogues, because for the most part those worshipers have become disillusioned and consider prayer an exercise in futility.

Most well-intentioned members of synagogue congregations are completely ignorant of the fact that *Kavanah* is the mainstay of our prayers. To attribute the drama of so-called miracles to the Lord of the Universe rather than to man's consciousness is a devastating corruption of Judaic belief. How often have we asked: Where was the Lord when I needed him most? How does the Lord choose his victims or survivors? Who determines which people shall be the *lucky* or *unlucky* ones? The Lord?

The answer, states the Zohar very emphatically, will be found in examining human activities, and this is where using the knowledge of the Kabbalah comes into play. With the proper *Kavanot* and the use of the seventy-two names,[139] Moses became the master of our corporeal, material realm. Armed with the awesome power of the Kabbalah,[140] the Red Sea no longer remained an obstacle for the Israelites.

We may believe that the events we encounter originate with the Lord or Lightforce. Nothing could be further from the truth.

The all-embracing unified whole, the Lightforce, has become shrouded in mystery as to its essential meaning. Consequently, service, worship and devotion have become menacing demonstrations of violence, mistrust, a right or wrong situation, and even murder, all for the sake of and in the name of the Lord. Of course, all this depends upon which suit of clothes or belief one might be clinging to at a particular time or age.

More than any other societal or political reason, this distortion, unfortunately, emerged concurrently with the establishment of varied religions and their offshoots — and there are so many. That is not to say that religion should not, or does not, exercise an important function in the development of human character.

However, somewhere, something went wrong. Along the way we began to assume the duties of the Lord's policemen. We developed the idea or ideas about what might be beneficial to our fellow man. From the intellectual arena, the notion of improving our neighbor or environment moved to the battlefield. If we failed to influence or convince others of our intent to enhance their lot, then we believed a more convincing approach to achieve the noble objective was to speak in the name of the Lord.

Failing in that attempt, we began waging war in the name of justice, or the Lord, without ever considering that it might never have been the Lord's intent to introduce suffering, pain and chaos as a solution to our problems. Examining the Lord's attributes should have sufficed in concluding that murder, no matter whether in the name of justice or the Lord, never could or would be sanctioned by the Lord.

The idea that the Lord favors some over others, raises the question of whether the Lord is partial and prejudicial. The Lord is not either of these. The Lord does not punish the infidels nor does He reward the faithful. The notion of reward and punishment, that the Lord rewards obedience and punishes the disobedient, is not contained in the teachings of Judaism. It is rather the thought and actions of mankind that result in the good and bad consequences which we think of as rewards and punishments.

Due to the doctrine of Bread of Shame, the Lord underwent

His own restriction. The restraint dictated that mankind must be provided with sufficient free will to achieve the purpose of Creation, namely the removal of Bread of Shame. The Lord does not interfere with this process. Consequently, the fulfillment of the effect of human activity was left to the Lord. So, depending on our behavior, the Lord carries out the results of our activity.

However, at the same time, the Lord knew at the outset that man would find the path leading to his objective strewn with obstacles and a maze of difficulties. He, therefore, provided the system of prayer by which mankind may overcome the impediments along the journey of life.

Aware of our natural tendency towards robotic consciousness, in which state the Dark Lord has the power to convince man of a sense of self-control while he is behaving robotically, the idea of *Kavanah* was established. *Kavanah*, and only *Kavanah*, states the Zohar, moves man from a robotic state of consciousness to one of mind control.

One of the simplest examples of how little control we exercise over the mind is found in the attempt to still the mind. Take a mere fifteen seconds of your time to relax and let the mind be still. I have found only a handful of people who can accomplish such a seemingly trivial feat without having thoughts flood the mind. This is the work of the Dark Lord, flooding us with thoughts to frustrate our period of silence. But, *Kavanah* is our answer.

The Dark Lord plays many tricks on us. For the most part he may bring us to a point of success, good health, exceptional relationships, having us believe we have accomplished these wonderful achievements on our own, independent of any outside assistance or influence.

Then, at a precise moment, when he believes he has ensnared us, all hell breaks loose. Suddenly, we find ourselves helpless, hopeless and without any notion of which direction to turn to. Our mind seems to go blank. The Dark Lord has even brought us to a point where we do not even question what has happened to our thinking ability. We do not question the fact that, if my ingenuity brought me to this point, how come the creative mind I supposedly possess does not serve me now or in this particular dilemma.

The Dark Lord is an excellent anesthesiologist. He has put mankind to sleep, although our egocentricity — another agent of the Dark Lord — finds this difficult to come to grips with. So many decisions are required each day, and *I* am the one making them. Doesn't this indicate that our brain or mind exercises control over our activities?

But, if we were asleep — the inference being that we were acting robotically — then those decisions or conclusions came about regardless of our conscious intervention. How many times have we taken long trips on superhighways and, after many hours of driving, realize that the past one or two hundred miles had gone by without our notice?

We can drive an automobile and yet permit our minds to wander elsewhere. This is equally true for persons who have been doing their daily prayers for years. They may only remember the opening prayer and unexpectedly they find themselves at the final prayer completely unaware of what transpired in between.

The purpose of *Kavanah* and consequently prayer itself, is to achieve an elevated state of consciousness and, in addition, to direct the mind toward that with which the mind must unite and merge. Elevating our consciousness simply means moving from our usual state of robotic consciousness to one where we take affirmative action, take our mind by the hand, and with our own initiative advise and command.

I am fully prepared for the probability of uncomplimentary responses to what has just been stated. We are all under the influence of the Dark Lord, who breeds his chaos and misfortune by imposing upon us a feeling of complacency, self-contentment, albeit only temporarily. The moment he understands that we have arrived at a self-assuring state of mind, the comfort of knowing that we are in control, he removes the rug from under us. The world comes tumbling down.

Our brain — so it seems — for some indeterminable reason no longer serves us well. Problems appear insurmountable threatening impending chaos and we find ourselves at a loss in coping with them. What happened? What brought about the shift from being a successful entrepreneur to a situation of bankruptcy and helplessness without any sign of hope on the horizon.

For a while, the Dark Lord retains his mastery over our minds and provides us with an infinite array of circumstances as to why it happened to "me". Our mind reflects upon and rationalizes the predicament we now find ourselves in, whether it is a financial matter, one of relationship, or a state of health that now seems to be in a chaotic condition for which we can find no solution. Once brought to our knees, the Dark Lord has no further need to continue his game, his purpose of manifesting chaos, and continues on to the next victim.

Behind this unfortunate scenario, declares the Zohar, lies the state of robotic consciousness known by the code name, Satan, Dark Lord. However, states the Zohar, were mankind involved in *Kavanah*, the system and exercise of directing and utilizing our mind, then the state of robotic consciousness would shift to an elevated state of awareness. We then would no longer experience the feeling of disappointment or abandonment.

The Dark Lord creates an atmosphere of materialism, exposure to the illusionary reality to which most human beings become addicted. The appearance and display of our physical world without consciousness might be compared to a body without a soul. We cannot have one without the other.

However, under no circumstances are we to consider the physical corporeal reality as our guiding force through the journey of life. The body is either dead or asleep when our consciousness becomes incapable of maneuvering our ship, the material physical body, to forge ahead towards the objective of fulfillment.

Without an active or determined consciousness, our ship or soul transporter flounders like an ocean liner on the high seas of storm and turmoil. Consequently, prayer with *Kavanah* serves as an activator and triggers our consciousness, the captain of our ship, to direct and navigate our lives with certainty through the murky waters of daily existence. This idea is strikingly expressed in the following Zohar.

> The Lord always delights in the prayer of the righteous and He crowns Himself with their prayers. As stated, the angel in charge of the prayers of Israel, Sandalphon by name, takes up all those prayers and weaves out of them a crown for the Lightforce. All the more so of the prayers of the righteous in which the Lord takes delight and are made into a crown for Him.

Seeing that Jacob had with him legions of holy angels,[141] it may be asked why he was afraid. The truth is that the righteous rely not on their merits but on their prayers to the Lightforce.

Rabbi Yehudah said: "Happy is the man that feareth always; but he that hardened his heart shall fall into evil."[142] To protect himself against Esau, Jacob resorted to prayer and did not rely upon his merit.

Observe that the prayer of other people [other than the poor] is just a prayer, but the prayer of a poor man breaks through all barriers and storms its way to the presence of the Lightforce.[143]

What seems to emerge from the Zohar are two significant revelations concerning the phenomenon known as prayer. Firstly, the delight in the Lightforce when prayers are directed to the Lightforce from the prayers of the righteous. This notion almost suggests that the Lord looks forward to and awaits the prayers. Of what need does the Lightforce have of these prayers?

But following the doctrine of "no coercion in spirituality"[144] the Lightforce cannot reveal its beneficence unless a need and proper vessel has been established by man. Consequently, the righteous ones, who have the knowledge and ability to state their prayers within a proper framework of *Kavanah*, prepare the vehicle by which the Lightforce can reveal Its beneficence.

Thus, the original "thought of Creation," that of sharing by the Lightforce, becomes manifested. The concept of Crowns adorning the Lightforce might be compared to the crowning of a king. Crowning of a king occurs only where a kingdom of the people exists. The righteous ones of the kingdom disclose the appearance of the Lightforce. In turn, the essential feature of the Lightforce, to share and pervade the universe, becomes a desired reality.

Therefore, prayers have a fundamental objective, to permit the universe to be filled with all the beneficence and positive energy of the Lightforce. In his desire to create a security shield to protect himself from Satan, the Dark Lord, portrayed by the code name Esau, Jacob created the channels, prayers by which he would be surrounded by the positive energy of the Lightforce.

For this very reason, he preferred not to depend on the "merit" of his forefathers, Abraham and Isaac, who were in a sense, also creators of prayer channeling. The totality of a three-column prayer structure would have to wait for its establishment by Jacob. Abraham represented the right column of energy-intelligence whereas Isaac created the prayer for placing left column energy-intelligence in our universe.

Secondly, Jacob may have been satisfied with the already established channels of energy-intelligence by his forefathers for the purpose of defending himself against the Dark Lord (his brother Esau).[145] However, he was aware that only a three-column system[146] could serve as his guarantee that no possible flaw might exist in his security shield. He consequently developed and expressed the central energy-intelligence force that stabilized and brought to pass a unity and circuitry between both right and left column energy-intelligences of his forefathers.

From the foregoing Zohar, it becomes crystal clear that prayer, from a Zoharic standpoint, is anything but the conventional idea of prayer. Its initial concept was established essentially to protect mankind from the accumulated activities of the devilish and threatening Dark Lord.

Another striking point presented in the Zohar is that the happiness of man is bound up and connected with those that "feareth always." Does this imply that one should constantly be fearful, nervous and full of anxiety? If so, how can the verse consider such an individual happy? When examining the underlying cause which produces fear in man, the uncertainty of what tomorrow will bring may be uppermost in our mind. The thoughts that we may lose our job, that ill health may befall us, that our relationships may be destroyed, could place us in a state of depression.

Given the circumstances under which most of us have chosen to play out our drama of *Tikune*, is it any wonder that many people are of a pessimistic frame of mind? To even suggest to many people, in this stress-filled age, that we have all the makings of our own unique fulfillment here, now, today, within ourselves — that we do not have to reach some financial or material goal or educational plateau to be complete — would produce a reaction of disbelief at best, and anger at being considered so gullible, at worst. Our dream home by the sea and all of the baubles of our illusionary fantasies, once acquired, will do little or nothing in and of themselves to make us happy and truly satisfied.

From the Kabbalistic perspective, merely acquiring more and more money and material possessions in hope of achieving happiness is like washing a car that is not running well and hoping that it would fix the motor; like polishing a rotten apple in the hope of making it fresh.

So what is the key to happiness and satisfaction in this

world? Being always in fear?

The answer lies with *Kavanah*. We are born with a metaphysical blueprint established in previous lives. This blueprint or karmic X-ray, includes illnesses as well as the power of healing those illnesses. Most of us live in robotic-consciousness that prevents us from making contact with the world of reality. This dark moment of a prior lifetime, governed by the Dark Lord, directs the day by day affairs of daily existence. To prevent an awareness of the game the Dark Lord plays with us, we are swept into a state of robotic consciousness, believing that important decisions concerning our daily routines are reached by our own consciousness.

We are the captain of our ship, master of our destiny, until such time in the *future* when we come to the realization that we no longer are the controller over our lives.

However, when prayer is accompanied by *Kavanah*, we begin to nurture and develop our mind to think for itself. The simple answer starts with the fear that we are not in control unless we tap the awesome power of the Lightforce, another example of the Kabbalistic use of paradox.[147] The paradox is that only by breathing out can we breathe in. By rejecting the Lightforce, one receives it. Having a fear that we are not in control welcomes and initiates opportunities for creative disengagement from the negative illusionary physical world, for by so doing we connect with the Infinite.

Resistance to the material illusion is the key to reality. Through the process of prayer and *Kavanah* one transcends the illusion established by the Dark Lord and creates a circuit with the alternate universe of the mind, thus becoming a channel for higher states of consciousness.

This is true control; this, not the tyranny of robotic-consciousness is the root of real self-determination and the way by which one establishes and connects with the Tree of Life Reality. If, however, one is led to believe that because he now possesses good health and this condition is eternal and everlasting, then the Dark Lord is truly his master.

However, if we come to the realization that at any given moment our entire world of happiness, contentment, financial security may crumble, and this kind of awareness is indeed one of *fear*, then we have no alternative but to follow the advice of the Zohar. If we make the most of Kabbalistic prayer with *Kavanah*, assuredly we shall connect and lock into the Lightforce.

When we are satisfied that we have all the wealth, health, and relationships that we desire, there is no room for the Light to enter. Should we recognize that it is possible for this situation to change, the element of fear enters. This fear should remind us to discontinue our birth-induced robotic-consciousness and rely instead on the Light.

Therefore, the Zohar cautions us, "happy is the man who always has fear." The Lightforce contains an uninterrupted desire to share. However, if there is no arousal for His beneficence or fulfillment, then the Lightforce is restricted in Its desire to impart to mankind. But once we have shifted our consciousness to a paradoxical image — that what we possess may not truly exist but is a temporary illusionary experience — then we direct our consciousnesss into that of lacking fulfillment rather than being in a state of fulfillment.

The resultant emptiness and lack of the Lightforce gives birth to an infinite desire to receive. We place ourselves in an incomplete state stretching out a hand to the Lightforce for support and assistance. The moment our desire to receive undergoes an arousal to receive, the Lightforce is there to fulfill our desires.

This is the reason for placing in man an unfulfilled desire to receive. The original Thought of Creation was only to impart the Creator's infinite beneficence, but we must learn how to construct the link between receiving and giving before we can bring that thought to completion.

The mystery of receiving, then, lies within the steady consciousness of being unfulfilled. This is true despite the deceptive influence of the Dark Lord who possesses every means of putting us to sleep. As a case in point, he might instill within us the thought that our health has never been better at a time when our body, unknown to us, is struggling to overcome an imbalance.

The Kabbalistic understanding of prayer will restore this balance and bring each one of us into harmony with the All-Embracing Unity of the Lightforce, and into "quantum consciousness." As we shall learn in Volume Two, Kabbalistic prayer is "Quantum Prayer."

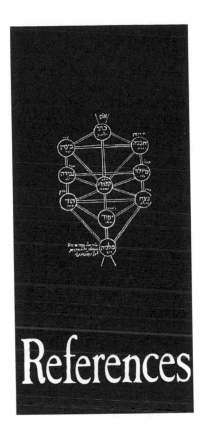

References

1. Zohar I, p.195b.
2. Talmud Bavli, Tractate Eruvin, p.45a; Tractate Gitin, p.78b, Tractate Bava Kama, p.116.
3. Power of Aleph Beth, Vol. I, Berg, pp.144-148.
4. Zohar III, p.287a.
5. Genesis 1:16.
6. Star Connection Berg, pp.40-41.
7. Kabbalah for the Layman, Vol. II, Berg, p.25.
8. Kabbalah for the Layman, Vol.I, Berg, pp.107-108.
9. Book of Formation, RCK edition, pp.102-106.
10. Time Zones, Berg, pp.168-169.
11. Star Connection, Berg, p.28.
12. Zohar I, p.24a.
13. Deuteronomy 6:4, 11:13.
14. Gates of Meditation, Vol.10, Kitvei Ari series, Rabbi

Isaac Luria, RCK, p.132.

15. Power of Aleph Beth, Berg, Vol.I.
16. Kabbalah for the Layman, Vol. I, Berg, pp.102-103.
17. Ibid.
18. Ibid.
19. Book of Formation, Research Centre of Kabbalah ed., Sec. 2,p.29.
20. Kabbalah for the Layman, Vol. II, Berg, pp.127-129.
21. Kabbalah for the Layman, Vol. III, Berg, p.61.
22. Power of Aleph Beth, Vol.I, Berg, p.78.
23. Power of Aleph Beth, Vol. I, Berg, pp.53-65.
24. Time Zones, Berg, pp.205-215.
25. Genesis 4:1.
26. Physics and Philosophy, Werner Heisenberg, p.177.
27. Dynamical Laws and Statistical Laws, Loudon, Taylor & Francis, 1972.
28. The Universe in the Light of Modern Physics, Planck.
29. Time Zones, Berg p.33.
30. Power of Aleph Beth, Berg Vol. 1, pp.174-175.
31. Kabbalah for the Layman, Berg, Vol. 1, pp.70-83.
32. Kabbalah for the Layman, Berg, Vol. II, pp.179-182.
33. Zohar III, p.149b.
34. Genesis 2:9.
35. Ibid., 2:16,17.
36. Zohar I, p.35b.
37. Proverbs 5:5.
38. Zohar III, p.23a
39. Jeremiah 31:33.
40. The Mysterious Universe, Sir James Jeans, AMS Press, reprint of 1933 edition.
41. Kabbalah for the Layman, Berg, Vol. III, p.90.
42. Kabbalah for the Layman, Berg, Vol. I, p.72.
43. Genesis 2:17.
44. Kabbalah Connection, Berg, pp.171, 172.

45. Star Connection, Berg, p.147, 158, 176.
46. Zohar III, p.23a.
47. Ibid., p.58a.
48. Ibid., p.95a.
49. Gates of Meditation, R. Isaac Luria, pp.310-313.
50. Genesis 4:7.
51. Zohar I, p.165 b.
52. Ecclesiastes 4:13.
53. Zohar I, p.179a
54. To the Power of One, Berg, pp.191-207
55. Zohar I, p.134 b.
56. Exodus 32:16.
57. Kabbalah for the Layman, Berg, Vol.III p.53-55.
58. Philosophy of Physics, Planck.
59. Tree of Life, Gate 1, Branch 2, Rabbi Isaac Luria, Kitvei Ari.
60. Ibid., 16a.
61. Kabbalah for the Layman, Vol III, Berg, pp. 71-75.
62. Zohar II, p.81a.
63. Exodus 20:15.
64. Isaiah, 52:8.
65. Genesis 11:1.
66. Zohar I, pp.74a-74b.
67. Genesis 15:5-6.
68. Kabbalah For The Layman, Berg, Vol. I, pp.71-74.
69. The Mysterious Universe, Sir James Jeans 1931, AMS Press Reprint.
70. Deuteronomy 6:4.
71. Talmud Bavli, Tractate Berakhot p.6b, Tractate Shabbat p.30b.
72. Exodus 19:20.
73. Power of Aleph Beth, Vol. I Berg, p.37.
74. Talmud Bavli, Tractate Shabbat, p.88b.
75. Talmud Bavli, Tractate Sanhedrin, p.90b.

76. Talmud Bavli, Tractate Shavuot, p.39a.
77. Leviticus 6:1,2.
78. Zohar III, p.26a.
79. Zohar III, p.26b.
80. Kabbalah for the Layman, Vol. II, Berg, pp.93,94.
81. Power of Aleph Beth Vol. I, Berg, pp.36,37.
82. Genesis 11:1.
83. Kings I, 6:7.
84. Zohar I, p.74a.
85. Genesis 11:2.
86. Genesis 11:6-8..
87. Genesis 11:6.
88. Zohar I, pp.74a-75b.
89. Power of Aleph Beth, Vol. 1, Berg. p.94.
90. Genesis 2:19.
91. Zohar I, p.97a.
92. Power of the Aleph Beth, Vol. I, Berg, pp.173-175,
93. Genesis 1:26.
94. Power of Aleph Beth, Berg, Vol. I, p.183-185.
95. Zohar I, p.134b.
96. Genesis 28:12.
97. Hovot ha-Levavot 8:3,9.
98. Isaiah 1:15.
99. Psalms 145.
100. Zohar III, p.183b.
101. Exodus 20:13.
102. Zohar I, p.17b.
103. Kabbalah for the Layman, Vol.1, Berg, pp.78-80.
104. Talmud Bavli, Tractate Gittin, p.7a.
105. Kabbalah for the Layman, Vol.III, Berg, p.116.
106. Genesis 28:12.
107. Zohar III, p.184b.
108. Talmud Bavli, Tractate Ber., 31a.
109. Ibid., 44a.

110. Ibid., Avot 2:13.
111. Ibid., Er., p.65a.
112. Zohar I, p.99b.
113. Zohar III, p.120b.
114. Zohar II, p.200a.
115. Zohar II, p.201a-201b.
116. Isaiah 49:3.
117. Genesis 1:16.
118. See Rabbi Ashlag's detailed explanations of The Twelve Letters.
119. Zohar II, p.201a-201b.
120. Deuteronomy 30:2.
121. Ibid., 30:4.
122. Zohar Hadash, Parashat Noah, p.23, Column 3.
123. Time Zones, Berg, pp.63-65.
124. Power of Aleph Beth, Vol. I. Berg, p.187-188.
125. Mishnah Yoma 6:2.
126. Talmud Bavli, Sotah, Mishnah 7:6.
127. Ibid., Tractate Kiddushin, p.71a.
128. Kabbalah for the Layman, Vol.I, Berg p.102.
129. Zohar III, p.78b.
130. Gate of the Holy Spirit, Gate of Meditations, Rabbi Issac Luria, Research Centre of Kabbalah.
131. Time Zones, Berg, p.115.
132. Kabbalah for the Layman, Vol.I, p.107.
133. Zohar III, p.122a.
134. Star Connection, Berg, pp.xvi, 21.
135. Hosea, 14:2,3.
136. Ezekiel 20:14.
137. Isaiah 48:9-11.
138. Zohar III, p.122a-122b.
139. Zohar II, p. 52a.
140. Exodus 14:19-21.
141. Genesis 32:2-7.

142. Proverbs 28:4.

143. Zohar I, p.168a-168b.

144. Ten Luminous Emanations, Ashlag, Vol. I, p.68 (1984 ed.).

145. Genesis 32:12.

146. Kabbalah for the Layman Vol.III, pp.141-142.

147. Kabbalah for the Layman, Vol.II, Berg, pp.161-164.

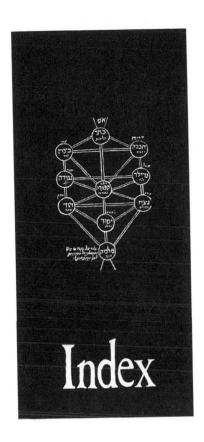

Index

KABBALISTIC ASTROLOGY MADE EASY
BY RABBI BERG

According to Kabbalah, the old adage, information is power, is incorrect. Information is not power. Knowledge is power. *Kabbalistic Astrology Made Easy* provides us with the precious knowledge of Judaic Astrology, helping us to surmount the onslaught of negativity that pervades our lives each month.

NEW RELEASE!!!

SECRET CODES OF THE UNIVERSE
BY RABBI BERG

The ultimate self-help book written by the renowned Kabbalist and author Rabbi Berg. Rabbi Berg explains in layman terms how to achieve personal success in all areas of our lives. Following his discourse, the reader will have the tools to begin a life journey filled with certainty and a new sense of purpose. Rabbi Berg brings the "old world" into the "new world" seamlessly and with a sensitivity seldom experienced in a book of this nature. Through the wisdom of ancient Jewish mystical thought, he allows the reader to finally get the answers to the "why" of the human experience. For those who want to regain control of their lives, this book is a "must read."

TO THE POWER OF ONE
BY RABBI BERG

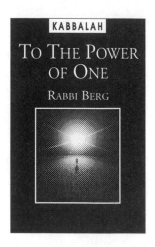

The universe, according to modern physics, is mysteriously interconnected as one unified whole by an invisible force that somehow reaches every corner of the cosmos. The ancient Kabbalists revealed these current scientific discoveries many centuries ago. They also asked questions: How does this information affect our lives right now on a practical level? In this book, we peer into the ancient wisdom of Kabbalah where the secrets of creation and human life have remained hidden for thousands of years. Rabbi Berg reveals a universe where the mind of God, human thought and the entire cosmos are interconnected as one.

WHEELS OF A SOUL
BY RABBI BERG

In this groundbreaking book, Rabbi Berg explores the Judaic process of reincarnation and the mysteries of the human soul. The judaic interpretations of life after death are truly fascinating, revealing provocative truths about the inner structure of Judaism. The reader gains profound insights into the many relationships that materialize in our lives including the areas of marriage and business. This important knowledge can help us resolve the difficult problems and obstacles that we confront on a daily basis.

KABBALAH
FOR THE LAYMAN
BY RABBI BERG

This comprehensive yet easily understood series traces the Kabbalah from its early beginning to the present day. Rabbi Berg demystifies Kabbalah, shedding new light on the laws that govern nature and the laws that govern human nature. We are given powerful tools to help us enhance, enrich and improve our lives in ways we never imagined. The inner chambers of Kabbalah are opened for all those who seek its profound wisdom and power.

TIME ZONE
BY RABBI BERG

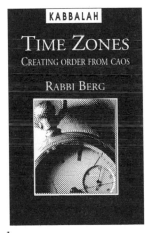

Time Zones provides the reader with the principles of Kabbalistic Astrology and its power in helping us overcome the struggle between failure and success. *Time Zones* gives us the precise knowledge about the best time to begin a marriage, start a new business, venture or engage in any new enterprise in our lives. Kabbalistic Astrology is the oldest and wisest application of this science known to man, not to be confused with conventional pop astrology and horoscopes we find in daily newspapers. Every holiday and significant date in Judaism is, in reality, an astrological event in the universe. Armed with this knowledge, we learn how to gain the advantage in every situation we face, every day of every year.

THE KABBALAH CONNECTION
BY RABBI BERG

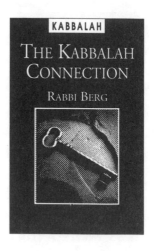

We are told by Kabbalah that for every blade of grass that grows here on earth there lies a corresponding influence among the stars in the universe. We can only then imagine the magnitude of influence affected by man... and by each individual person. Explore the interconnectedness of our universe in the *Kabbalah Connection* and discover the ancient formula for awakening good fortune, inner peace and fulfillment in our day to day lives.

POWER OF THE ALEPH BETH
BY RABBI BERG

The Hebrew letters, according to Kabbalah, are the formulas for 22 energy forces that were active in the creation process prior to the appearance of our universe as we know it today. The letters of the Hebrew Aleph Beth are the DNA code of the cosmos. Understanding the individual and combined powers of the Aleph Beth helps us to connect to the primordial energy of creation which can then help us remove the chaos and disorder that permeates our lives.

THE STAR CONNECTION
BY RABBI BERG

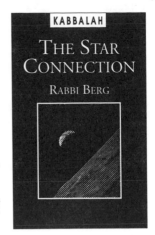

This compelling book pours a clear light onto the concealed reasons why certain events appear in our lives and the world at large. Exploring the ancient principles of Kabbalistic Astrology, *The Star Connection* reveals that each of us is born into an astrological environment best suited for the completion of the correction that we must make in our lives.

GIFT OF THE BIBLE
BY RABBI ASHLAG

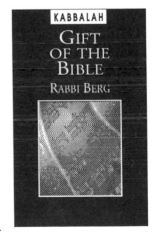

A simple yet profound book offering a Kabbalistic perspective on the world around us. Rabbi Yehuda Ashlag possesses a rare gift - the ability to take even the most advanced and complex principles and reduce them to a simple equation of truth that can be understood by all.Experience the Gift of the Bible and discover the true power of Kabbalah.